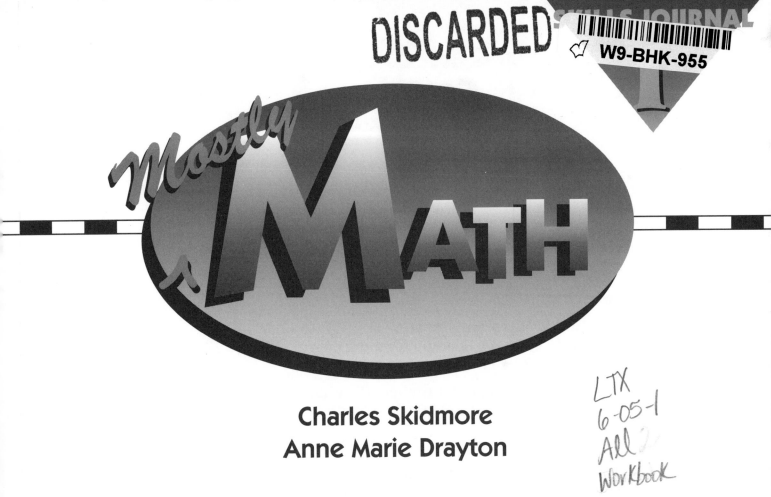

Mostly MATH

Charles Skidmore
Anne Marie Drayton

Addison-Wesley Publishing Company

ISBN 0-201-88088-1
Complete Skills Journal: Mostly Math, Mostly Science, Mostly Social Studies

3 4 5 6 7 8 9 10 -CRS- 00 99 98 97

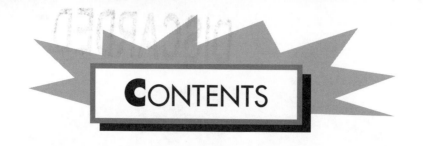

CONTENTS

Mostly Math Skills Journal   3–32
(To accompany student pages 3–32)

• •

Featuring:

A Publication of the World Language Division

Director of Product Development: Judith M. Bittinger
Executive Editor: Elinor Chamas
Editorial Development: Kathleen M. Smith
Text and Cover Design: Taurins Design Associates
Art Direction and Production: Taurins Design Associates
Production and Manufacturing: James W. Gibbons

Illustrators: Chris Reed 6, 16, 17, 20, 23; Dave Sullivan 9, 32

• •

Number, Please

Answer the following questions. Each answer will be a number.

1. How old are you? _____

2. How many brothers and sisters do you have? _____

3. How many students are in your class? _____

4. How many students are in your school? _____

5. How many languages do you speak? _____

6. How many countries have you lived in? _____

7. How many books do you read each year? _____

8. How many states are there in the United States? _____

9. How many days are there in a week? _____

10. How many sides does a triangle have? _____

11. How many hours do you sleep every night? _____

12. How many minutes are there in an hour? _____

13. How many days are there in the month of December? _____

14. How many planets are there? _____

15. How many years are there in a century? _____

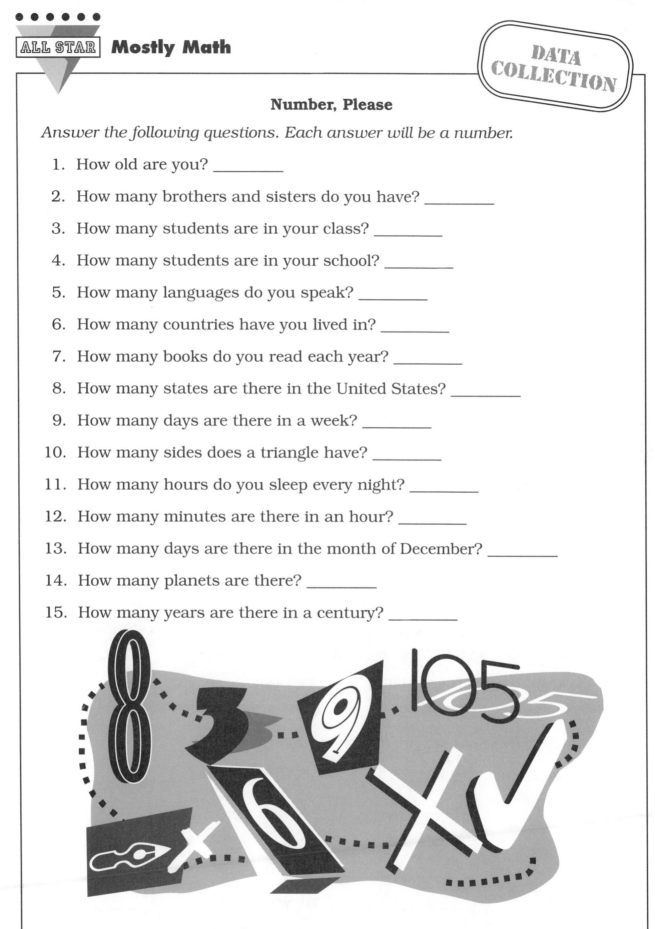

(Supports Mostly Math magazine) **Home-School Connection; data collection; research; writing numbers.**
Students may need to look for some answers in a dictionary or encyclopedia. Have them complete the page
independently or with a partner. Have students take this page home to share with their families.

Forming the Plural

> Most nouns in English form the **plural** by adding *-s*.
>
> **Examples:** letter/letter<u>s</u>   name/name<u>s</u>   animal/animal<u>s</u>

A. *Add -s to these words. The first one is done for you.*

1. bed	*beds*	11. house	_____
2. book	_____	12. map	_____
3. boy	_____	13. name	_____
4. car	_____	14. notebook	_____
5. chair	_____	15. paper	_____
6. computer	_____	16. pen	_____
7. desk	_____	17. pencil	_____
8. dog	_____	18. room	_____
9. eye	_____	19. school	_____
10. girl	_____	20. teacher	_____

> Nouns that end in *-s, -sh, -ch,* and *-x* form their **plurals** by adding *-es*.
>
> **Examples:**   rush/rush<u>es</u>   tax/tax<u>es</u>

B. *Add -es to these words. The first one is done for you.*

1. beach	*beaches*	6. dress	_____
2. box	_____	7. fox	_____
3. brush	_____	8. glass	_____
4. church	_____	9. lunch	_____
5. dish	_____	10. watch	_____

4

(Supports Mostly Math magazine, pages 4–6) **Plurals with *-s* and *-es*; spelling.** Students complete the page independently. Check answers in class. You may want to save this page in the student's **Assessment Portfolio.**

More Plurals

> Some English words have **spelling changes** in the plural forms.
> They change the last letter -*y* to -*i* and add -*es*.
>
> **Examples:** ci*ty*/cit*ies*   par*ty*/part*ies*

A. *Make these words plural. Change -y to -i and add -es. The first
one is done for you.*

1. baby   *babies*   5. family   _____

2. country   _____   6. lady   _____

3. dictionary _____   7. library   _____

4. fairy   _____   8. story   _____

> Some words have **special plural forms**. Study these
> words and their plurals.
>
> | child | children | | mouse | mice |
> |-------|----------|--|--------|--------|
> | foot | feet | | person | people |
> | goose | geese | | tooth | teeth |
> | man | men | | woman | women |

B. *Write a sentence using each plural word.*

children_____

_____

feet _____

_____

people _____

_____

women _____

_____

(Supports Mostly Math magazine, pages 4–6) **Plurals with -*ies* and irregular plurals; spelling.** Students complete the page independently. Check answers in class. You may want to save this page in the student's
Assessment Portfolio.

Whales, Rabbits, Foxes

A. *Look at the information about three different animals.*

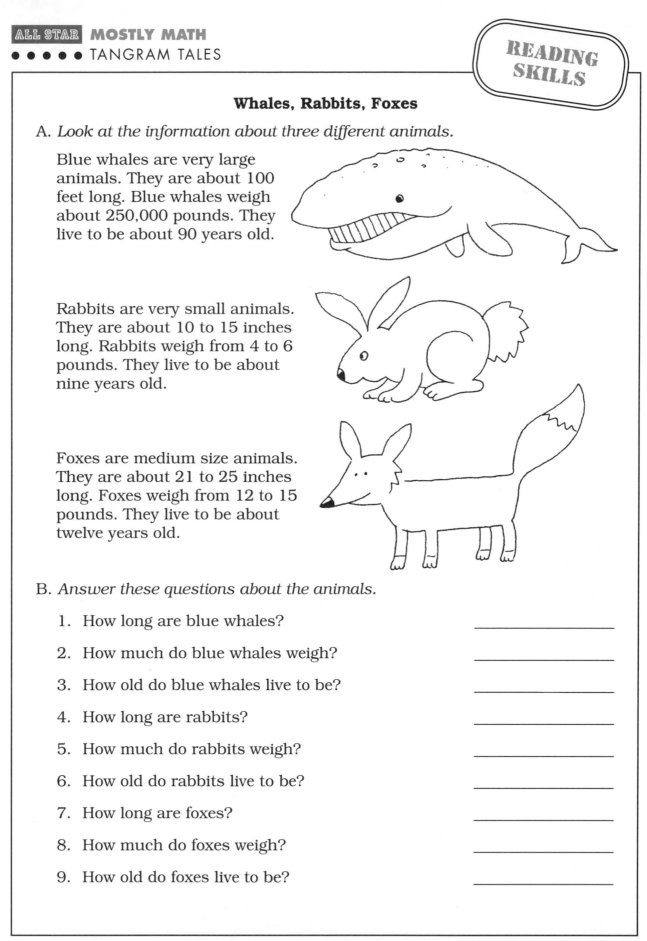

Blue whales are very large animals. They are about 100 feet long. Blue whales weigh about 250,000 pounds. They live to be about 90 years old.

Rabbits are very small animals. They are about 10 to 15 inches long. Rabbits weigh from 4 to 6 pounds. They live to be about nine years old.

Foxes are medium size animals. They are about 21 to 25 inches long. Foxes weigh from 12 to 15 pounds. They live to be about twelve years old.

B. *Answer these questions about the animals.*

1. How long are blue whales? _____

2. How much do blue whales weigh? _____

3. How old do blue whales live to be? _____

4. How long are rabbits? _____

5. How much do rabbits weigh? _____

6. How old do rabbits live to be? _____

7. How long are foxes? _____

8. How much do foxes weigh? _____

9. How old do foxes live to be? _____

(Supports Mostly Math magazine, pages 4–6) **Reading comprehension; learning *inches, pounds, years*; compare and contrast.** Students can work with a partner to complete the page. For more work, have students write complete sentences on another piece of paper for the answers in Exercise B. Check answers in class. You may want to save this page in the student's **Assessment Portfolio.**

Design Your Own Flag Alphabet

A. *You can write secret codes to your friends! Design an alphabet where each letter is a different flag or symbol.*

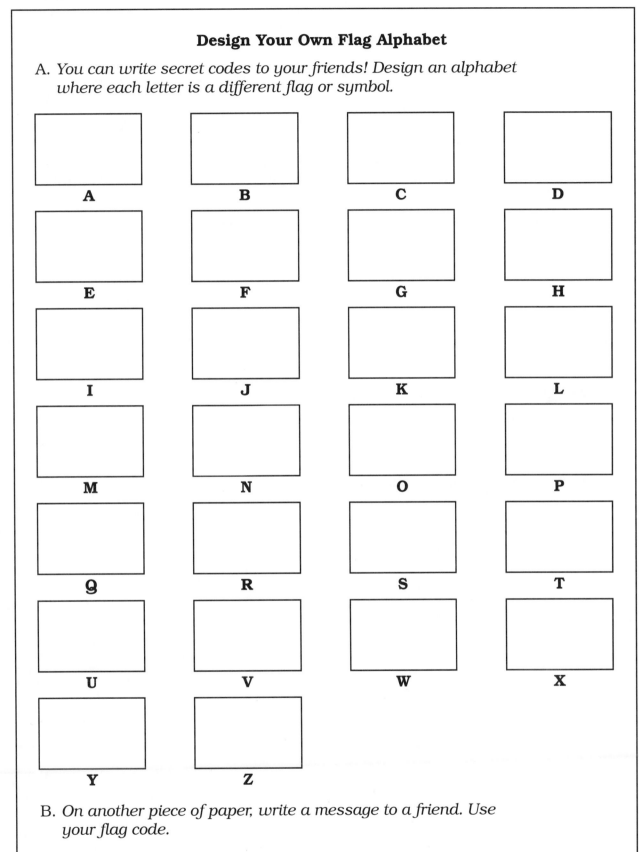

B. *On another piece of paper, write a message to a friend. Use your flag code.*

(Supports Mostly Math magazine, page 7) **Imagery; creating a secret code; language appreciation.** Have volunteers show their flag alphabets to the class. Encourage partners to exchange messages with their codes.

7

Shapes and Prepositions

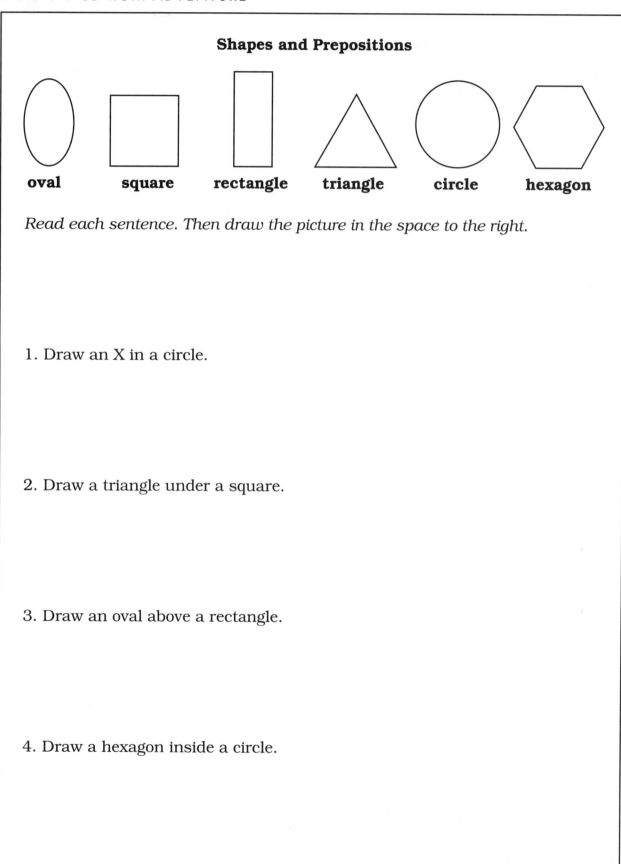

oval   square   rectangle   triangle   circle   hexagon

Read each sentence. Then draw the picture in the space to the right.

1. Draw an X in a circle.

2. Draw a triangle under a square.

3. Draw an oval above a rectangle.

4. Draw a hexagon inside a circle.

© Addison-Wesley Publishing Company

(Supports Mostly Math magazine, pages 8–9) **Drawing shapes; prepositions of place; following directions.**
Students complete the page independently. Check answers in class. For more work, have students make a list
of the prepositions in the directions.

The Dangerous Sun

A. *Read the paragraphs about the sun.*

Captain ROM and Byte visit the Shapes Universe. They see many numbers and shapes on the beach. They are lying in the sun. Many people on Earth do this, too. They go to the beach. They play in the sun. They lie on the sand. Many people with light skin want their skin to be darker. This is called "getting a tan."

Getting a tan hurts our skin. We should not work or play in the sun without protection. If we do, we may get skin cancer after many years. What can you do to save your skin? You can wear sunscreen every day. You can also try to stay out of the sun when it is the strongest. That's between about 11:00 a.m. and 3:00 p.m.

B. *Read each statement. Write* **True** *or* **False** *on the line.*

1. Many people play in the sun at the beach.   _____

2. Many people with light skin want their skin to be lighter.   _____

3. "Getting a tan" means that skin gets darker.   _____

4. Getting a tan is good for our skin.   _____

5. If we work and play in the sun, we may get skin cancer after many years.   _____

6. We can protect our skin by wearing sunscreen.   _____

7. The sun is hottest between 4:00 p.m. and 8:00 p.m.   _____

(Supports Mostly Math magazine, pages 8–9) **Reading for a purpose; learning about the sun; writing.**
Students can read the story aloud with a partner. Check answers to Exercise B in class. You may want to save this page in the student's **Assessment Portfolio.**

Colors

A. *Read the paragraphs about colors.*

The three primary colors are red, yellow, and blue. Other colors come from mixing these three colors. Green is a mixture of yellow and blue. Purple is a mixture of red and blue. Orange is a mixture of yellow and red.

Many colors can combine to make other colors. White and red together make pink. Red, blue, and white together make lavender. You can use white to make other colors lighter.

B. *Answer these questions about colors.*

1. What are the three primary colors?

_____

2. What two colors together make green?

_____

3. What happens if you mix red and blue together?

_____

4. How do you make orange?

_____

5. How do you make lavender?

_____

C. *Use a red, a yellow, and a blue colored pencil to color these shapes.*

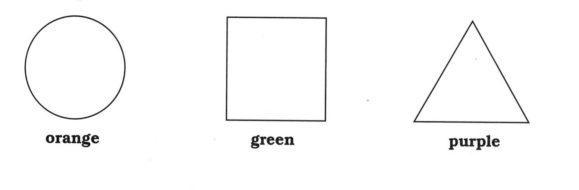

orange   **green**   **purple**

© Addison-Wesley Publishing Company

(Supports Mostly Math magazine, page 10) **Colors; shapes; reading for a purpose; writing.** Students can read the selection aloud with a partner. Check answers to Exercise B in class. You may want to save this page in the student's **Assessment Portfolio.**

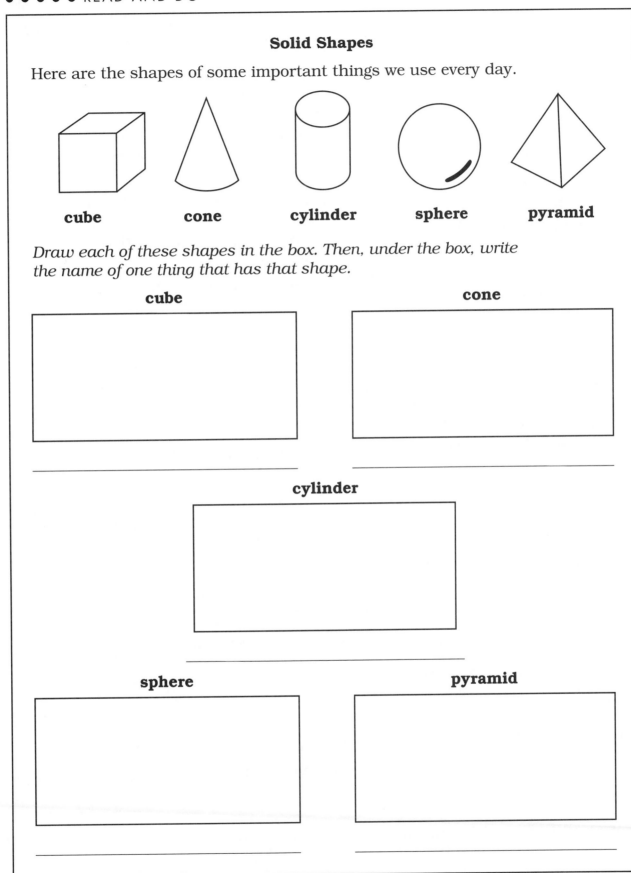

Solid Shapes

Here are the shapes of some important things we use every day.

cube   cone   cylinder   sphere   pyramid

Draw each of these shapes in the box. Then, under the box, write the name of one thing that has that shape.

cube

cone

cylinder

sphere

pyramid

(Supports Mostly Math magazine, page 11) **Home-School Connection; shapes; brainstorming.** Students complete the page independently. Make a list for the class of all the items the students name in their boxes. Have students take this page home to share with their families.

READING SKILLS

Math Terms

You need to know many important math terms. Here are some of them.

decrease - to make or get smaller

even number - any number that can be divided by two without a remainder

equation - a number sentence; $5 = 5 = 10$ is an equation

exponent - a number that shows how many times a number should multiply itself; 2^5 means $2 \times 2 \times 2 \times 2 \times 2$ and equals 32

increase - to get larger

multiplication table - a list that shows the multiplication of a certain number by the numbers 1–12. The multiplication table for 7 is

7 x 1 = 7	7 x 7 = 49
7 x 2 = 14	7 x 8 = 56
7 x 3 = 21	7 x 9 = 63
7 x 4 = 28	7 x 10 = 70
7 x 5 = 35	7 x 11 = 77
7 x 6 = 42	7 x 12 = 84

negative number - a number less than zero. For example, -23 is a negative number.

odd number - any number that cannot be divided by 2 evenly. For example, 23 is an odd number.

positive number - any number greater than zero. For example, 23 is a positive number.

square root - a number multiplied by itself to get another number; 6 is the square root of 36 because $6 \times 6 = 36$. The symbol for square root is $\sqrt{}$.

Learn these square roots.

$\sqrt{1} = 1$	$\sqrt{49} = 7$
$\sqrt{4} = 2$	$\sqrt{64} = 8$
$\sqrt{9} = 3$	$\sqrt{81} = 9$
$\sqrt{16} = 4$	$\sqrt{100} = 10$
$\sqrt{25} = 5$	$\sqrt{121} = 11$
$\sqrt{36} = 6$	$\sqrt{144} = 12$

Answer these questions. Use the math terms to help you.

1. What is the square root of 64? _____

2. What is 3^4? _____

3. What is 8 times 1? What is 8 times 12? _____

4. Write a negative number and a positive number. _____

5. Is 75 an odd or an even number? _____

6. Are these numbers increasing or decreasing? 4, 8, 12, 16 _____

(Supports Mostly Math magazine, pages 12–13) **Math terms; problem solving.** Students study the definitions before answering the questions. Check answers in class. For more work, have students answer the questions in complete sentences on another piece of paper.

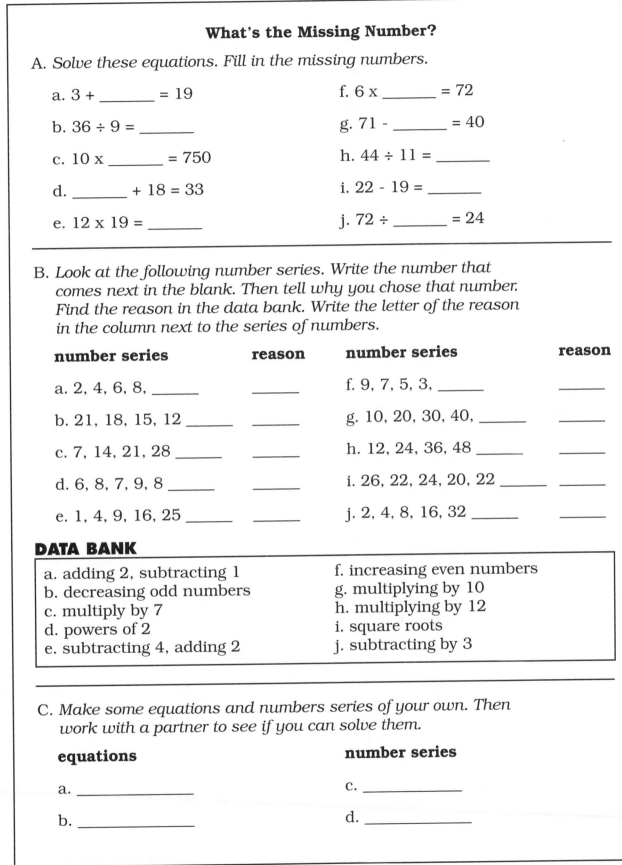

What's the Missing Number?

A. *Solve these equations. Fill in the missing numbers.*

a. 3 + _____ = 19

b. 36 ÷ 9 = _____

c. 10 x _____ = 750

d. _____ + 18 = 33

e. 12 x 19 = _____

f. 6 x _____ = 72

g. 71 - _____ = 40

h. 44 ÷ 11 = _____

i. 22 - 19 = _____

j. 72 ÷ _____ = 24

B. *Look at the following number series. Write the number that comes next in the blank. Then tell why you chose that number. Find the reason in the data bank. Write the letter of the reason in the column next to the series of numbers.*

number series	reason	number series	reason
a. 2, 4, 6, 8, _____	_____	f. 9, 7, 5, 3, _____	_____
b. 21, 18, 15, 12 _____	_____	g. 10, 20, 30, 40, _____	_____
c. 7, 14, 21, 28 _____	_____	h. 12, 24, 36, 48 _____	_____
d. 6, 8, 7, 9, 8 _____	_____	i. 26, 22, 24, 20, 22 _____	_____
e. 1, 4, 9, 16, 25 _____	_____	j. 2, 4, 8, 16, 32 _____	_____

DATA BANK

a. adding 2, subtracting 1
b. decreasing odd numbers
c. multiply by 7
d. powers of 2
e. subtracting 4, adding 2

f. increasing even numbers
g. multiplying by 10
h. multiplying by 12
i. square roots
j. subtracting by 3

C. *Make some equations and numbers series of your own. Then work with a partner to see if you can solve them.*

equations

a. _____

b. _____

number series

c. _____

d. _____

(Supports Mostly Math magazine, pages 12–13) **Equations and number series; problem solving.** Students complete Exercises A and B independently. Check in class. Have students do Exercise C with a partner. Volunteers can share their equations and number series with the class.

13

Percent

Percent shows a certain part of 100. Study this word problem to see how to calculate percent.

Miguel bought three books for $5.00 each. The sales tax was 5%. How much tax did he pay?

Step 1. Find out how much money Miguel spent.
Multiply 3 x $5.00. He spent $15.00.

Step 2. Find out how much tax he paid. ($\frac{5}{100}$ represents the percent of tax)

Set up the equation: $\frac{5}{100}$ x $\frac{x}{15}$
Cross multiply: 5 x 15 = 75
Divide by 100: 75 ÷ 100 = .75

Miguel paid $.75 in tax.

Solve these percent problems. Do the work on another piece of paper. Write the answers here.

1. The Perez family went to a restaurant. They celebrated their daughter's fifteenth birthday. The bill was $150 for the dinner. They wanted to leave the waitress a 20% tip. How much did they leave for a tip? _____

2. Tim and Keisha bought a new refrigerator for $700. The sales tax was 5%. How much tax did they pay? _____

3. Martin is buying a guitar from a friend. The guitar costs $80.00. He is paying 50% this month and 50% next month. How much is Martin paying each month for the guitar? (Hint: 50% = one half) _____

4. The Young Saver Bank is paying 8% interest per year on student savings accounts. Sara is putting $400 in the bank for a year. How much interest will the bank pay her at the end of a year? _____

5. Kim is buying a bicycle with some money she earned from washing cars on the weekends. The bicycle costs $95. The sales tax is 8%. How much tax does she have to pay? _____

(Supports Mostly Math magazine, pages 14–15) **Percents; reading word problems.** Go over the example with students before you assign the exercise. Check answers in class. For more work, have students make up a percent problem of their own to exchange with a partner and solve.

How Much?

A. *These are orders placed at Mike's Munchy Meals Restaurant. Write the price next to each item. Add them to find the subtotal. Then figure 5% tax on the subtotal. Write the total on the last line. Use the prices on page 14 in the magazine. The first one is done for you.*

1.

Mike's Munchy Meals	
1 Chicken taco	1.29
1 cole slaw	1.19
1 med. lemonade	.99
1 cookie	1.39
Subtotal	4.86
5% tax	.24
Total	5.10

2.

Mike's Munchy Meals	
2 Veggie burgers	
1 corn dog	
2 tomato salads	
2 sm. iced teas	
Subtotal	
5% tax	
Total	

3.

Mike's Munchy Meals	
1 Buffalo burger	
1 order plantains	
1 lg. soda	
1 chocolate pudding	
Subtotal	
5% tax	
Total	

4.

Mike's Munchy Meals	
1 med. iced tea	
1 lg. lemonade	
2 sm. sodas	
4 orders curly fries	
Subtotal	
5% tax	
Total	

B. *Now make up your own orders. Figure out how much the total is.*

1.

Mike's Munchy Meals	
Subtotal	
5% tax	
Total	

2.

Mike's Munchy Meals	
Subtotal	
5% tax	
Total	

(Supports Mostly Math magazine, pages 14–15) **Percents; filling in forms.** Students complete the page independently. Check answers in class.

15

Math Term Check-Up

See how many of the math terms you know. Label as many as you can. Check with your teacher or partner to see how you did.

(Supports Mostly Math magazine, pages 16–17) **Math terms; labeling pictures.** You may want to review pages 16 and 17 in the Mostly Math magazine before assigning this page. Students complete the page independently. Check answers in class.

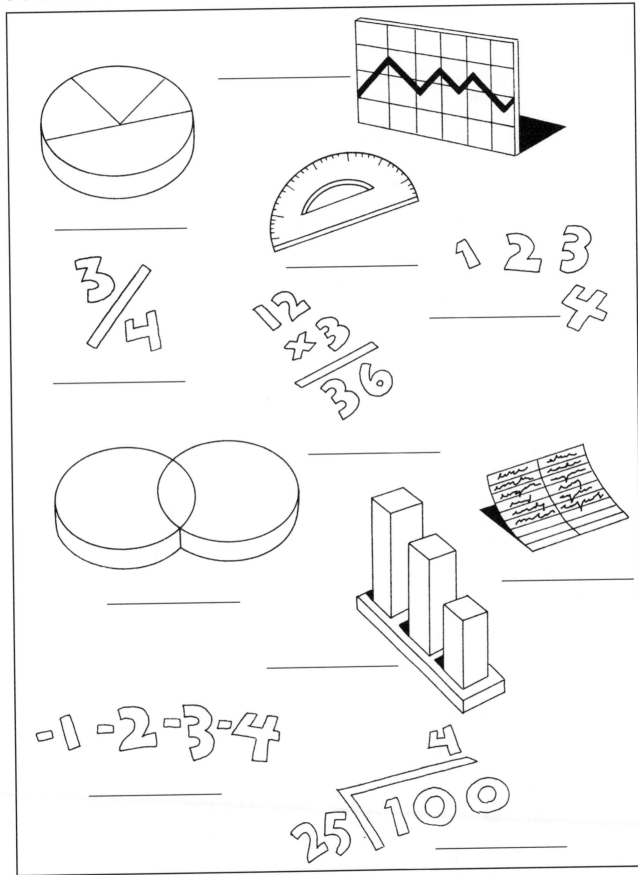

(Supports Mostly Math magazine, pages 16–17) **Math terms; labeling pictures.** You may want to review pages 16 and 17 in the Mostly Math magazine before assigning this page. Students complete the page independently. Check answers in class.

17

Fractions

A **fraction** shows a part of a whole. The top number of a fraction is called the **numerator.** It shows how many parts of the whole are being talked about. The bottom number is the **denominator.** It tells the total number of parts.

Example: $\dfrac{1}{2}$ numerator denominator

Look at the pictures. Write a fraction for each picture. Follow the examples.

Examples:

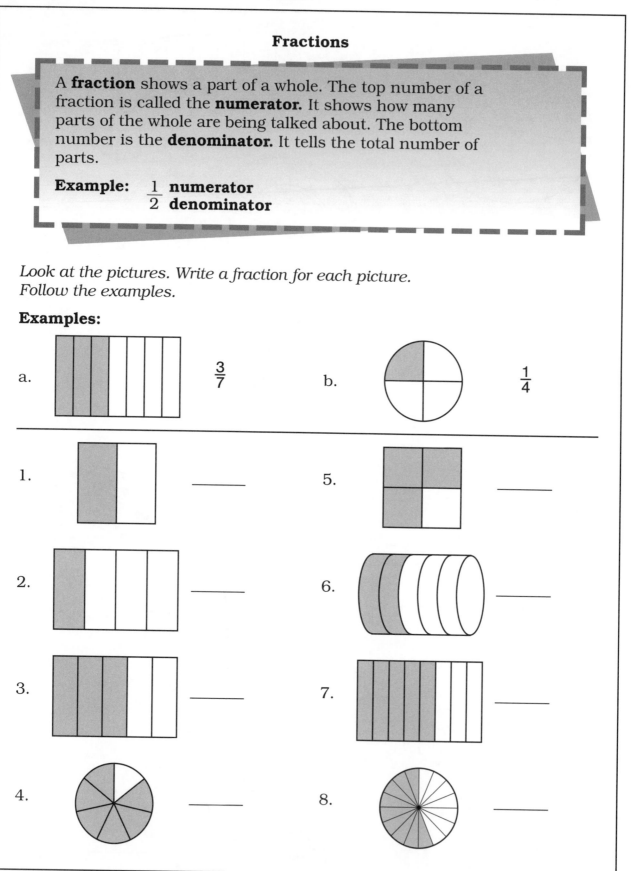

a. $\dfrac{3}{7}$

b. $\dfrac{1}{4}$

1. _____

2. _____

3. _____

4. _____

5. _____

6. _____

7. _____

8. _____

(Supports Mostly Math magazine, pages 18–19) **Fractions; shapes; problem solving.** Students complete the page independently. Check answers in class.

Reducing Fractions to Lowest Terms

In a fraction, the numerator and the denominator should always be at their **lowest terms.** To reduce a fraction to its lowest terms, divide the numerator and the denominator by the same number.

Examples:

$$\frac{4}{6} \begin{array}{l} \text{(divide by 2)} \\ \text{(divide by 2)} \end{array} = \frac{2}{3} \textbf{ lowest terms}$$

$$\frac{6}{18} \begin{array}{l} \text{(divide by 6)} \\ \text{(divide by 6)} \end{array} = \frac{1}{3} \textbf{ lowest terms}$$

Reduce these fractions to their lowest terms. Write the new fraction on the line.

1. $\frac{2}{4}$ = _____

2. $\frac{5}{25}$ = _____

3. $\frac{2}{8}$ = _____

4. $\frac{3}{21}$ = _____

5. $\frac{8}{16}$ = _____

6. $\frac{4}{32}$ = _____

7. $\frac{7}{21}$ = _____

8. $\frac{9}{18}$ = _____

9. $\frac{10}{100}$ = _____

10. $\frac{20}{40}$ = _____

11. $\frac{3}{99}$ = _____

12. $\frac{8}{24}$ = _____

13. $\frac{9}{33}$ = _____

14. $\frac{6}{32}$ = _____

15. $\frac{4}{18}$ = _____

16. $\frac{25}{100}$ = _____

17. $\frac{17}{51}$ = _____

18. $\frac{8}{20}$ = _____

19. $\frac{14}{26}$ = _____

20. $\frac{12}{48}$ = _____

(Supports Mostly Math magazine, pages 18–19) **Fractions: lowest terms; problem solving.** Students complete the page independently. Check answers in class.

19

Brown Bears

A. *Read the paragraphs about brown bears.*

Brown bears, like Magda and Josef, live in Europe, Asia, and North America. Brown bears can be very different in size. Some brown bears in Spain weigh only about 450 pounds. Brown bears in Alaska can weigh more than 1,550 pounds!

Brown bears are omnivorous. This means that they eat meats and plants. Brown bears eat other animals, insects, honey, fruit, and grass. In the fall, brown bears get fatter. When winter comes, they find a cave to live in. There they spend the winter. They sleep and live off the fat in their bodies.

B. *Read these statements. Write* **True** *or* **False** *on the line.*

1. Brown bears live in Europe, Asia, and North America. _____

2. Brown bears in Alaska weigh about 450 pounds. _____

3. An omnivorous animal eats meat and plants. _____

4. Brown bears eat other animals, insects, honey, fruit, and grass. _____

5. Brown bears lose fat in the fall. _____

6. They spend the winter in trees. _____

(Supports Mostly Math magazine, pages 20–23) **Reading for a purpose; learning about bears.** Students can read the story aloud with a partner. Check answers to Exercise B in class. For more work, have students rewrite the false statements as true. You may want to save this page in the student's **Assessment Portfolio.**

Weights and Measures

A. *Look at the following chart. Read the weights and measures.*

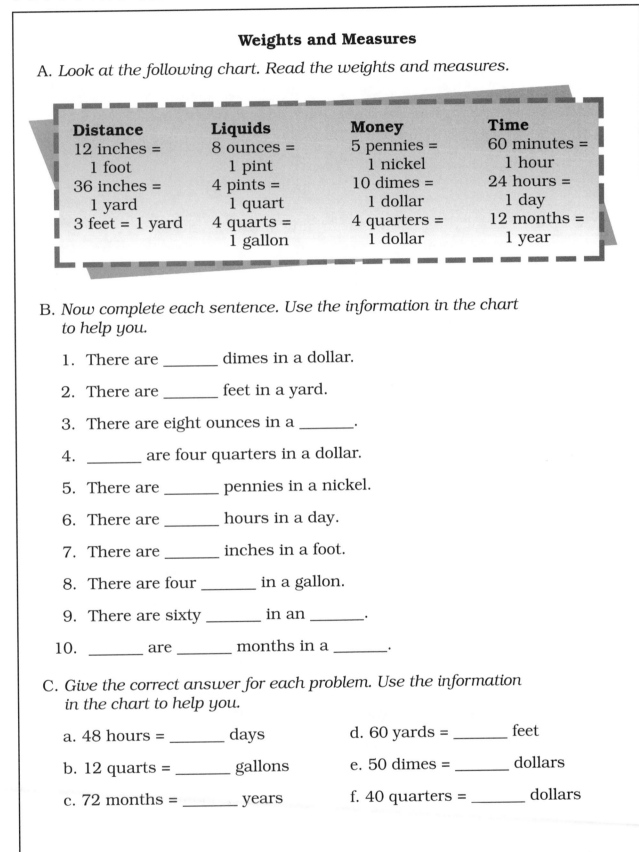

Distance	Liquids	Money	Time
12 inches = 1 foot	8 ounces = 1 pint	5 pennies = 1 nickel	60 minutes = 1 hour
36 inches = 1 yard	4 pints = 1 quart	10 dimes = 1 dollar	24 hours = 1 day
3 feet = 1 yard	4 quarts = 1 gallon	4 quarters = 1 dollar	12 months = 1 year

B. *Now complete each sentence. Use the information in the chart to help you.*

1. There are _____ dimes in a dollar.

2. There are _____ feet in a yard.

3. There are eight ounces in a _____.

4. _____ are four quarters in a dollar.

5. There are _____ pennies in a nickel.

6. There are _____ hours in a day.

7. There are _____ inches in a foot.

8. There are four _____ in a gallon.

9. There are sixty _____ in an _____.

10. _____ are _____ months in a _____.

C. *Give the correct answer for each problem. Use the information in the chart to help you.*

a. 48 hours = _____ days

b. 12 quarts = _____ gallons

c. 72 months = _____ years

d. 60 yards = _____ feet

e. 50 dimes = _____ dollars

f. 40 quarters = _____ dollars

(Supports Mostly Math magazine, pages 20–23) **Weights and measures; problem solving, syntax.** Students can work with a partner to complete the page. Check answers in class.

21

Close to Exact

Sometimes you can figure out problems by **estimating** the answer. When you estimate, you find a number that is close to the exact number. Study this example.

Estimate the answer to this problem: 299 + 105.

Step 1. Change 299 to 300 by rounding up to the nearest hundred.

Step 2. Change 105 to 100 by rounding down to the nearest hundred.

Step 3. Add the two numbers: 300 + 100 = 400.
The estimated answer is 400. The exact answer is 299 + 105 = 404. The estimated answer is close to the exact answer.

A. *Estimate the answers to these problems. Do not use a calculator. First round each number up or down. Then do the math. Write your answer on the line.*

Problem	**Work space**	**Estimated answer**
1. 497 + 399		_____
2. 19 x 59		_____
3. 789 + 404		_____
4. 611 + 598 + 701		_____
5. 7,129 + 2,979		_____

B. *Sometimes when you estimate you guess about how much. Give your estimates for the following information.*

1. Estimate the number of words you know in English. _____

2. Estimate the number of hours of homework you do every week. _____

3. Estimate the hours of television you watch in a month. _____

(Supports Mostly Math magazine, pages 20–23) **Estimating; solving problems; guessing.** Have students study the information in the box before you assign the rest of the page. For more work, have students compute the exact answers to the problems in Exercise A. Students can share their guesses in Exercise B with the class.

Two Pieces of Cheese

You need to know special serving words to talk about different foods. Here is a list of serving words and food.

Serving word	Food
a scoop of	ice cream
a head of	lettuce
a bag of	chips, pretzels
a pound of	cheese, meat
a piece of	cake, toast
a stick of	butter
a bowl of	cereal
a slice of	pizza, pie
a can of	tuna, beans
a box of	crackers, cereal

Sometimes you talk about more than one serving. Make the serving word plural, not the food word.

Example: Enrico has a piece of cheese on his plate. (three)
Enrico has three <u>pieces</u> of cheese on his plate.

Make the serving word in each sentence plural. Rewrite the whole sentence.

1. I want to buy a head of lettuce. (three)

_____

2. My sister ate a scoop of ice cream. (four)

_____

3. Claudia bought a can of tuna. (two)

_____

4. Marie wants a slice of pizza for lunch. (two)

_____

5. Billy had a piece of toast for breakfast. (three)

_____

© Addison-Wesley Publishing Company

(Supports Mostly Math magazine, pages 20–23) **Food serving words; plurals; spelling.** Assign the page after students have studied the words in the list and the examples. For more work, have students write sentences using the plurals of serving words in the list that are not used in the exercise. You may want to save this page in the student's **Assessment Portfolio.**

Word Relationships

An **analogy** is a word relationship. In an analogy, the relationship between two sets of words is the same.

Example: triangle: 3 :: rectangle: _____

Read the analogy this way: *Triangle is to 3 as rectangle is to _____.*

The answer is 4 because a triangle has three sides and a rectangle has 4 sides. This analogy shows a relationship between the names of the shapes and the number of sides.

Complete these analogies. Write the correct word in the blank.

1. numerator: top :: denominator: _____
   a. number   b. fraction   c. math   d. bottom

2. foot: 12 :: yard: _____
   a. inches   b. 36   c. measure   d. mile

3. whale: big :: rabbit: _____
   a. small   b. animal   c. quick   d. tangram

4. child: children :: tooth: _____
   a. bite   b. tongue   c. mouth   d. teeth

5. taco: eat :: lemonade: _____
   a. food   b. sweet   c. drink   d. Mexican

6. cat: kitten :: bear: _____
   a. animal   b. cub   c. forest   d. honey

7. positive: negative :: plus: _____
   a. number   b. good   c. minus   d. addition

8. odd: 7 :: even: _____
   a. never   b. 24   c. number   d. 9

(Supports Mostly Math magazine, page 24) **Analogies; reading.** Students complete the page independently. Check answers in class.

Positive and Negative Numbers

Positive numbers, like 2 and 25, show a value of 0 or more.
Negative numbers, like -2 and -25, show a value of less than 0.
When you hear that the temperature is -15°, you know it's cold!

In business, a positive number shows how much money was made in one year. This money is called a **profit**. A negative number shows how much money was lost. It is called a **loss.**

A. *Look at the line graph. It shows the profits and losses for Five Corners Software Company. Study the graph.*

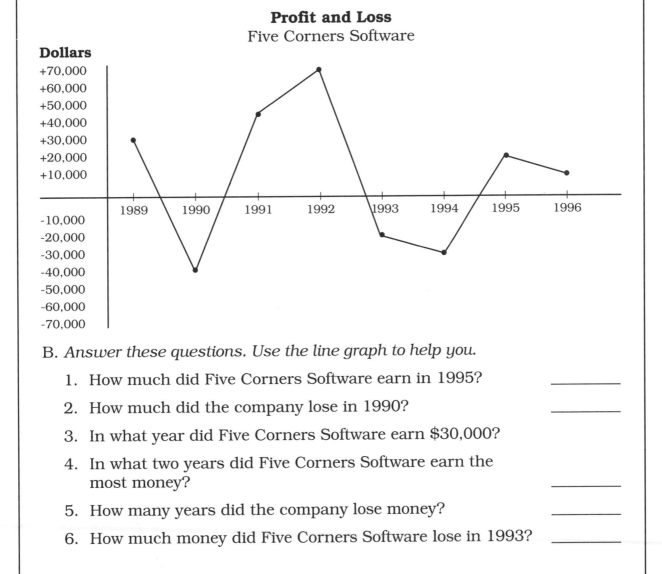

Profit and Loss
Five Corners Software

B. *Answer these questions. Use the line graph to help you.*

1. How much did Five Corners Software earn in 1995? _____

2. How much did the company lose in 1990? _____

3. In what year did Five Corners Software earn $30,000?

4. In what two years did Five Corners Software earn the most money? _____

5. How many years did the company lose money? _____

6. How much money did Five Corners Software lose in 1993? _____

(Supports Mostly Math magazine, page 25) **Positive and negative numbers; reading a line graph.** Before assigning Exercise B, make sure students understand *positive number, negative number, profit, and loss.* Check the answers to Exercise B in class. For more work, have students make up an imaginary company and create figures for a profit and loss line graph.

PROCESS WRITING

You and Your Money

A. *Read the paragraphs about money and kids.*

     Everyone needs and uses money. Money can be a big problem for young people. Some kids are too young to get jobs. In many states, you have to be at least 16 to get a job. Sometimes, kids under 16 can find neighborhood jobs. These can be babysitting, mowing lawns, or shoveling snow.
     Some parents give kids money when they do work around the house and yard. The kids might take out the trash, feed the family pet, or do the dishes.
     How does your family share money?

B. *Complete the graphic organizer. Tell how you spend your money.*

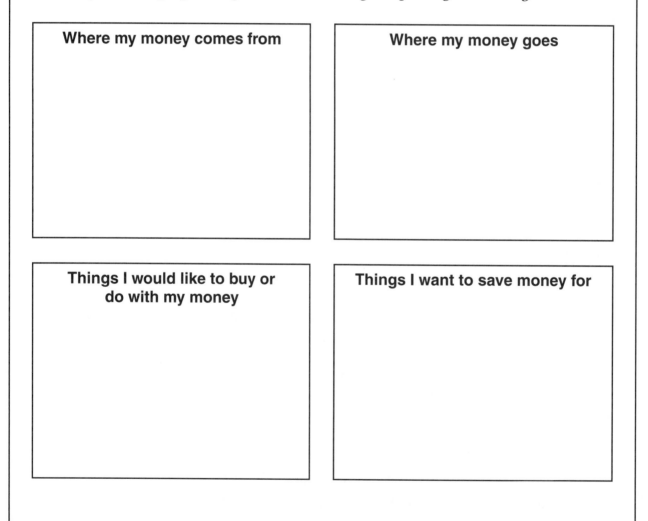

Where my money comes from	**Where my money goes**
Things I would like to buy or do with my money	**Things I want to save money for**

(Supports Mostly Math magazine, page 26) **Home-School Connection; reading for a purpose; brainstorming; process writing.** After students read the story, lead a discussion about how their families share money. Volunteers can share their information in Exercise B with the class. For more work, suggest that students write a few paragraphs about how they spend their money. Have students take this page home to share with their families.

Money to Spend!

A. *Imagine that you had $500 to spend on anything you want. What would you do with the money? Follow these steps to help you decide. Fill in the chart below.*

1. **Brainstorm.** Make a list of several things you want to buy or do.
2. **Estimate.** Write the amount that you think each item will cost.
3. **Prioritize.** In the last column in the chart, put a number 1 next to the item you want most. Put a number 2 beside the item you want next, and so on. This is called prioritizing. It means you are deciding what is most important to you.

Brainstorming list— what I want to buy	Estimated cost	Priority rank

B. *How many of your items can you afford? Follow these steps to fill in the chart on the next page.*

1. **Make a new list.** List the items from the first chart. This time, put them in the order that you ranked them. Write the estimated cost of each item.
2. **Calculate.** Add the estimated cost of all the items. Is the total more or less than $500? How many of your items can you afford?
3. **Get feedback (other people's opinions).** Share your list with a partner. What does you partner think about your list? What things are on your partner's list. Are any items the same on both lists?

(Supports Mostly Math magazine, page 27) **Expressing opinions about money; filling in charts; adding; estimating costs.** Students can brainstorm their lists with a partner in Exercises A and B. Make sure they understand the meanings of *prioritize, estimate, calculate,* and *feedback.*

Prioritized list	Estimated cost

Total _____

C. *Read the statements. Put a check next to the ones that are true about you and money.*

1. I like to spend my money on myself.

2. I like to share my money with my family.

3. I like to use my money to help others.

4. I like to save all my money for the future.

5. I like to spend some money and save some money.

6. I like to spend money on experiences (movies, travel, etc.).

7. I like to spend money on things (clothes, games, books, etc.).

8. I like to spend money on education (art or music lessons, save for college, etc.).

(Supports Mostly Math magazine, page 28) **Prioritizing a list, expressing opinions about money.** Have students share their prioritized lists with the class. Encourage discussion about the items they checked in Exercise C.

Fact or Opinion

A **fact** is a true statement that you can prove.
An **opinion** is a feeling or belief that someone has. Here are some words people use when they express an opinion: *good, bad, boring, stupid, best, delicious, awful.*

A. *Read each statement. Write* **fact** *or* **opinion** *on the line.*

1. A triangle has three sides. _____

2. The English alphabet has 26 letters. _____

3. English is the best language in the world. _____

4. Bears are bad animals. _____

5. Math is a very boring subject. _____

6. There are three feet in a yard. _____

7. Blue and yellow mix to make green. _____

8. Tangrams is a stupid game. _____

9. The numerator is the top number in a fraction. _____

10. Cheese sandwiches are delicious. _____

11. The United States is about 3,000 miles wide. _____

12. The number 7 is the best number. _____

13. The United States has 50 states. _____

14. Purple is an ugly color. _____

15. The sun is 93,000,000 miles away from Earth. _____

B. *On another piece of paper, write some facts and opinions of your own. You can write about people, places, math, television, sports, or anything you want.*

(Supports Mostly Math magazine, page 29) **Fact vs. opinion.** Students complete the page independently or wit a partner. Have students share their statements in Exercise B. You may want to save this page in the student's **Assessment Portfolio.**

29

Math Poem

Write your own poem about numbers. It can be about your family, your class, animals, or anything else that can be about numbers. Use the poems on page 30 of the Mostly Math magazine as a model.

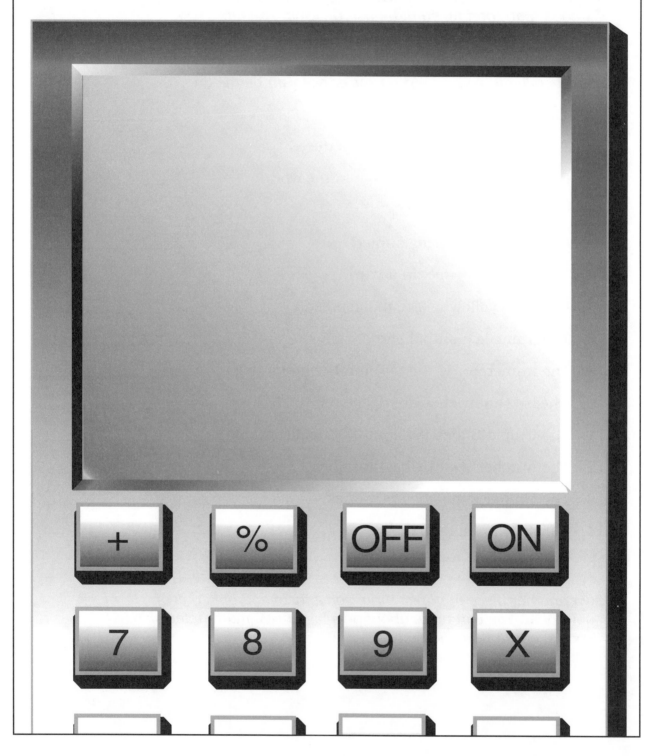

(Supports Mostly Math magazine, page 30) **Writing a poem; creativity with numbers.** Have volunteers share their poems with the class. You may want to save this page in the student's **Assessment Portfolio.**

Sidney's Saturday

Sidney wanted to keep track of how he spent his time on one day of the weekend. He chose Saturday.

A. *Study the list to see what Sidney did on Saturday.*

Time	Activity
7:00–8:00	1. got dressed, took a shower, ate breakfast
8:00–11:00	2. played basketball at school
11:00–12:00	3. talked with friends
12:00–1:00	4. ate lunch, washed dishes
1:00–3:00	5. volunteered at the hospital
3:00–5:00	6. did homework
5:00–6:00	7. ate dinner, fed my dog
6:00–7:00	8. babysat my little brother
7:00–10:00	9. watched TV with friends
10:00–7:00	10. slept

B. *The pie chart shows 24 hours in the day. How many hours did Sidney spend on each activity? Fill in the right number of wedges with the number of each activity. The first one is done for you.*

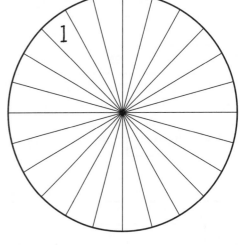

C. *Answer the questions. Use Sidney's list and the pie chart to help you.*

1. When did Sidney take care of his little brother? _____

2. How many hours did Sidney spend playing basketball? _____

3. How many hours did he volunteer at the hospital? _____

4. When did he watch TV with friends? _____

5. How many hours did he spend on homework? _____

6. How many 1-hour activities did Sidney have? _____

7. What activity took the longest time? _____

(Supports Mostly Math magazine, page 31) **Home-School Connection; filling in a pie chart; understanding fractions.** Students can work with a partner or independently to complete page. For more work, have students keep track of their activities for one day and fill in a list and pie chart like the ones on this page. Have students take this page home to share with their families.

© Addison-Wesley Publishing Company

HOW ARE YOU DOING?

Now I Can	yes	no	not sure
1. collect data			
2. use graphic organizers			
3. form regular and irregular plurals			
4. draw circles, squares, triangles, and rectangles			
5. use primary colors to make other colors			
6. understand the difference between fact and opinion			
7. use food serving words			
8. reduce fractions to lowest terms			
9. answer questions about brown bears			
10. estimate answers to problems			

Now I Know	In My Language	yes	no	not sure
cheese				
color				
computer				
equation				
every				
eye				
flag				
lunch				
money				
rabbit				
salad				
skin				
square				
triangle				
weekend				

____ Teacher Check

(Supports Mostly Math magazine) **Home-School Connection; self-assessment, vocabulary development.** Students fill in the grids about what they have learned in this magazine. In the bottom grid, suggest that students write each vocabulary word in their native language in the blank column. You may want to save this page in the student's **Assessment Portfolio**. Have students take a copy of this page home to share with their family members.

Pond Life

A. *Derek, Marcia, Felicia, and Victor each did a report on two pond creatures. Read the clues. Which students studied each animal? Put checks in the table.*

Clues

1. The same girl reported on sunfish and ducks.
2. Each of the boys reported on different spiders.
3. Marcia reported on the crayfish.
4. The person who reported on the land spiders also reported on the otters.
5. Victor reported on the beavers.

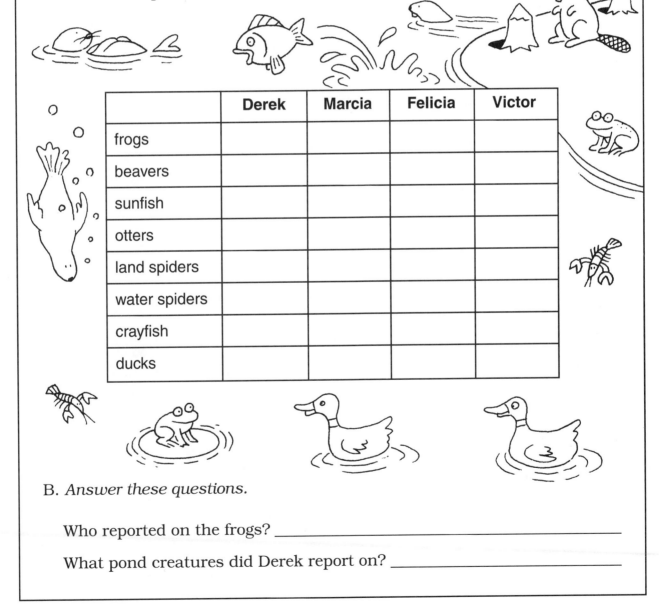

	Derek	Marcia	Felicia	Victor
frogs				
beavers				
sunfish				
otters				
land spiders				
water spiders				
crayfish				
ducks				

B. *Answer these questions.*

Who reported on the frogs? _____

What pond creatures did Derek report on? _____

(Supports Mostly Science magazine, pages 4–6) **Logical thinking; filling in a chart.** Students can complete the page independently or with a partner. Check answers in class.

5

Word Search Puzzle

A. *This puzzle contains words about beavers and their world.*
Read the list of words below. Find the words in the puzzle and
circle them.

```
I C H E W W I D E E S H
M U D A N G E R B L R C
Y D H L D C D H S T E Q
D S D M I O A N E S M H
S C U K V A P H E I M M
E L H B E A T A R H I H
H O A F L F O B T W W R
C D B S R E V A E B S E
N G I H B O T T O M E D
A E T P I K P O N D O N
R K A M T E E T H H K U
B H T F F B I B U R P N
```

BEAVER	DANGER	POND	TEETH
BOTTOM	DIVE	RUB	TREES
BRANCHES	HABITAT	SLAP	UNDER
BUSY	LODGE	SWIMMERS	WHISTLE
CHEW	MUD	TAIL	WIDE

© Addison-Wesley Publishing Company

(Supports Mostly Social Studies magazine, pages 4–6) **Solving a puzzle; pond habitat words; spelling; socializing.** Students can work individually or in pairs to solve the puzzle. Check in class.

Symmetry

Objects that have symmetry are all around us. Symmetry means that an object is the same or equal on both sides of a line or around a center. Here are some examples of symmetry.

A. *Design your own symbol. It can be for yourself, your family, your school, your team, or anything else that is important to you. Make your symbol an object of symmetry.*

B. *Present your symbol to the class. Describe it. Then tell why you chose it and what it means to you.*

(Supports Mostly Science magazine, page 7) **Home-School Connection; understanding symmetry; learning through art.** Have partners check each other's symbols for symmetry. Allow time for students to present their symbols to the class. Have students take this page home to share with their families.

READING SKILLS

More About Magnets

A. *Read the paragraphs about magnets.*

We use magnets in all kinds of machines. You can find magnets inside refrigerator doors and telephones. Magnets are also in electric motors, food mixers, and drills.

Every magnet has a north pole and a south pole. Two north poles or two south poles push each other apart. We say that two poles of the same kind **repel** each other.

One north pole and one south pole pull each other together. We say that different poles **attract** each other. That means they pull together.

B. *Answer the questions about magnets.*

1. Where can you find magnets?

    _____

2. How many poles do magnets have?

    _____

3. What happens when you put two north poles together?

    _____

4. What happens when you put two south poles together?

    _____

5. What happens when you put a north pole and a south pole together?

    _____

(Supports Mostly Science magazine, pages 8–9) **Reading for a purpose; learning about magnets; writing.** If necessary, preview the words *repel* and *attract.* Students can read the story aloud with a partner. Have them complete Exercise B independently. Check answers in class. You may want to save this page in the student's **Assessment Portfolio.**

Big, Bigger, Biggest

Short words use **-er** and **-est** to show comparison.

Examples: Florida is <u>bigger</u> than Vermont.
This tree is the <u>tallest</u> one in the park.

A. *Label the pictures with the correct form of the adjective. Follow the example.*

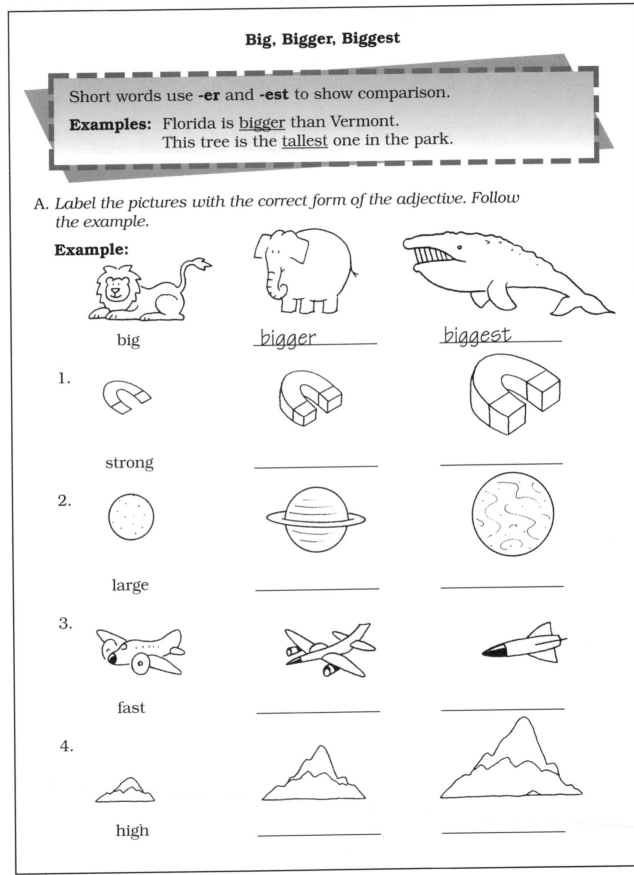

Example:

big   bigger   biggest

1.

strong   _____   _____

2.

large   _____   _____

3.

fast   _____   _____

4.

high   _____   _____

(Supports Mostly Science magazine, pages 8–9) **Comparative adjectives with** *-er* **and** *-est*; **spelling; learning through art.** Students complete the page independently. Check in class. You may want to save this page in the student's **Assessment Portfolio.**

Opposites

A. *Study these pairs of opposite words with a partner. On another piece of paper, draw a picture or write a sentence that shows what each word means.*

big - small	old - young	dark - light
long - short	wide - narrow	above - below
full - empty	quiet - noisy	right - left

B. *Circle the correct word in parentheses.*

1. Eight cars can fit on this highway. It is very (narrow/wide).

2. An airport is a (noisy/quiet) place when an airplane is landing.

3. I ate so much food. I am (full/empty).

4. The student raised his hand (above/below) his head.

5. The mother beaver taught the (old/young) beavers to swim.

6. In English we read from the (right/left) side of the page.

7. Texas is a (big/small) state.

8. An underground cave is very (dark/light).

9. Lee's hair was (short/long) after the barber cut it.

C. *Match the words in column A to their opposites in column B. Put the correct letter on the line. You may need to use a dictionary.*

A	**B**
1. friend _____	a. sick
2. healthy _____	b. rough
3. smooth _____	c. sour
4. sweet _____	d. enemy
5. top _____	e. bottom

(Supports Mostly Science magazine, page 10) **Opposites; syntax, using a dictionary.** Encourage students to share their sentences and drawings in Exercise A. Check Exercises B and C in class. Have students look up unfamiliar words. You may want to save this page in the student's **Assessment Portfolio.**

Homophones

Some words in English sound the same but have different spellings. These words are called **homophones**.

Example: hear/here

A. *Study these homophones with a partner. On another piece of paper, draw a picture or write a sentence that shows what each word means.*

write - right	their - there	too - to - two
peace - piece	here - hear	meet - meat
hi - high	sea - see	sun - son

B. *Circle the correct homophone in parentheses.*

1. Do you have a (peace/piece) of paper I can use?

2. Beavers live (here/hear) in the summer.

3. I like (too/to/two) play tangrams with my grandfather.

4. Tom will (write/right) a letter to his friend later.

5. The girls are looking for (their/there) sneakers in the gym.

6. All the planets move around the (sun/son).

7. You can't (sea/see) the mountains when it's cloudy.

8. I like vegetables more than I like (meet/meat).

9. That (hi/high) building blocks out the sun.

C. *Each of these words has a homophone partner. It's a word that sounds the same but has a different spelling. Work with a partner and write the homophone partner for each word.*

blue _____	new _____	some _____
eight _____	red _____	week _____

© Addison-Wesley Publishing Company

(Supports Mostly Science magazine, page 11) **Homophones; syntax, using a dictionary.** Encourage students to share their sentences and drawings in Exercise A. Check Exercises B and C in class. Have students look up unfamiliar words. You may want to save this page in the student's **Assessment Portfolio.**

CD ROM and Big Toe

A. *Write the number 1 next to the first thing that happened in the story. Write number 2 next to the next thing that happened, and so on.*

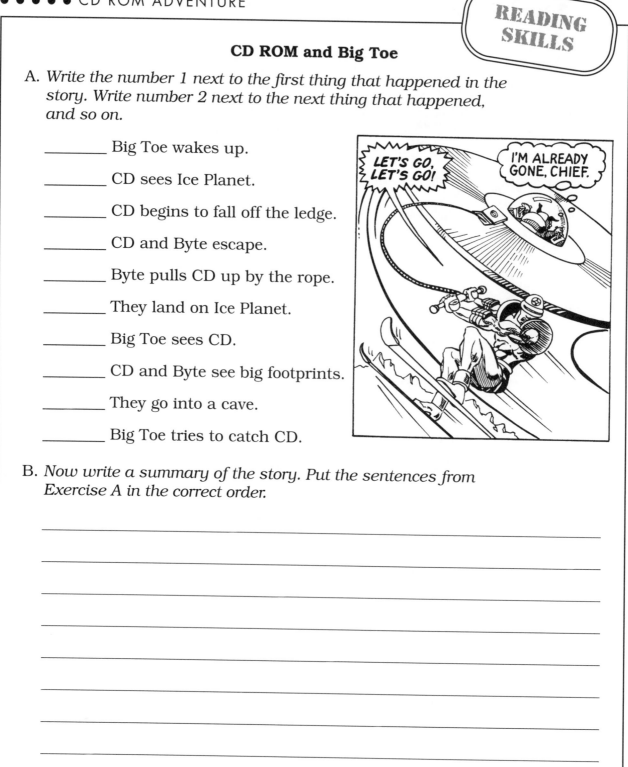

_____ Big Toe wakes up.

_____ CD sees Ice Planet.

_____ CD begins to fall off the ledge.

_____ CD and Byte escape.

_____ Byte pulls CD up by the rope.

_____ They land on Ice Planet.

_____ Big Toe sees CD.

_____ CD and Byte see big footprints.

_____ They go into a cave.

_____ Big Toe tries to catch CD.

B. *Now write a summary of the story. Put the sentences from Exercise A in the correct order.*

_____

_____

_____

_____

_____

_____

_____

_____

_____

_____

(Supports Mostly Science magazine, pages 12–13) **Story sequence; writing a summary.** If necessary review what a *summary* is. Students complete the page independently. Check in class. You may want to save this page in the student's **Assessment Portfolio.**

Experiment With Ice

What makes ice melt? Does it always melt at the same speed?

Materials:
- two ice cubes
- two shallow dishes

A. *Observe and collect data.*

1. Put an ice cube in each of two shallow dishes.
2. Place one dish in a shaded area. Place the other dish in a sunny area.
3. Time how long it takes each ice cube to melt.
4. Then hold an ice cube in your hand. Time how long it takes the ice cube to melt.

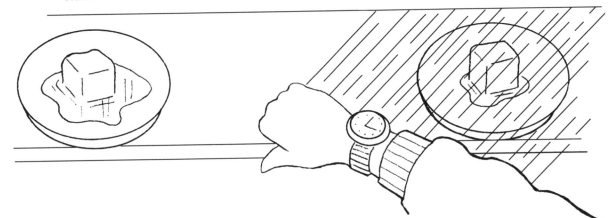

B. *Draw conclusions.*

Compute and compare the melting times. What are your conclusions? Write them here.

_____

_____

_____

_____

_____

_____

_____

© Addison-Wesley Publishing Company

(Supports Mostly Science magazine, pages 12–13) **Data collection; conducting an experiment; measuring time; comparing and contrasting.** Students work with a partner to complete the page. Have them compare their results with the rest of the class.

Loud Sounds, Soft Sounds

A. *Fill in the graphic organizer with as many sounds as you can think of.*

Loud sounds	Soft sounds

Sounds I like	Sounds I don't like

B. *Write a sentence about your favorite sound.*

_____

_____

_____

(Supports Mostly Science magazine, pages 14–15) **Brainstorming sounds; process writing; expressing opinions.** Students complete the page independently. Have students compare their lists of sounds. For more work, have students write a sentence about each sound in their graphic organizer.

Adjectives With *More* and *Most*

Long words use **more** and **most** to show comparison.

Examples: Julia is <u>more athletic</u> than Raoul.
Apples are the <u>most delicious</u> fruit in the world!

A. *Fill in the blanks with <u>more</u> and <u>most</u> comparisons.*
Follow the example.

Example:

beautiful	*more beautiful*	*most beautiful*
1. powerful	_____	_____
2. dangerous	_____	_____
3. popular	_____	_____
4. intelligent	_____	_____
5. difficult	_____	_____
6. interesting	_____	_____
7. careful	_____	_____
8. delicious	_____	_____

B. *Write a sentence using each comparative adjective.*

1. more popular

_____

2. more interesting

_____

3. the most dangerous

_____

4. the most powerful

_____

(Supports Mostly Science magazine, pages 14–15) **Comparative adjectives with *more* and *most*; syntax, spelling.** Students complete the page independently. Have students compare their lists of sounds. For more work, have students write a sentence about each sound in their graphic organizer. You may want to save this page in the student's **Assessment Portfolio.**

Science Term Check-Up

See how many of the science terms you know. Label as many as you can. Check with your teacher or partner to see how you did.

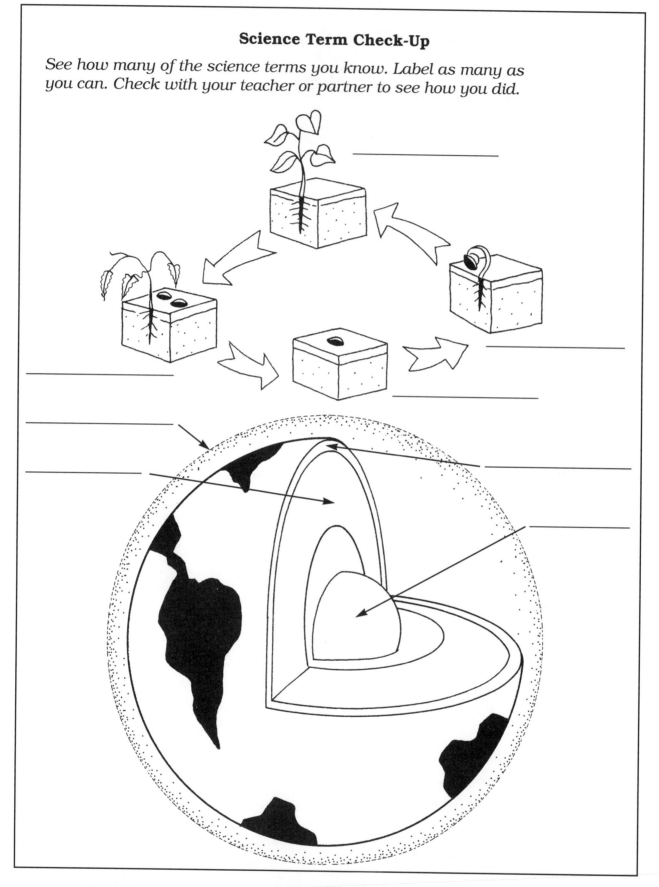

(Supports Mostly Science magazine, pages 16–17) **Science terms; labeling pictures.** You may want to review pages 16 and 17 in the Mostly Science magazine before assigning this page. Students complete the page independently. Check answers in class.

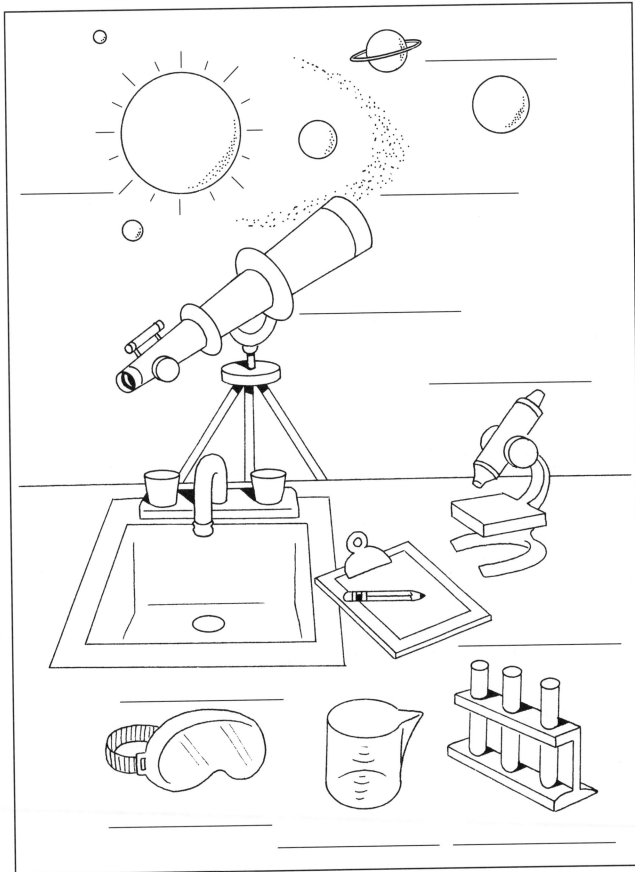

(Supports Mostly Science magazine, pages 16–17) **Science terms; labeling pictures.** You may want to review pages 16 and 17 in the Mostly Science magazine before assigning this page. Students complete the page independently. Check answers in class.

Food Chains

A. *Read about food chains.*

Many animals eat grass. Other animals eat the grass-eaters. Then other animals eat the animal-eaters. A simple food chain can go like this:

| Grass. | A rabbit eats the grass. | A fox eats the rabbit. |

or like this:

| Grass. | A cow eats the grass. | A human eats the cow. |

Green plants make their own food from water, soil, and sunlight. Animals spend a lot of time looking for food. They eat plants. They get energy from plants.

B. *Read each statement. Write **True** or **False** on the line.*

1. Some animals eat grass.   _____

2. Other animals eat the grass-eaters.   _____

3. No animals eat the animal-eaters.   _____

4. In a simple food chain, animals eat only grass.   _____

5. Green plants make food from moonlight.   _____

6. Animals that eat plants get energy from plants.   _____

© Addison-Wesley Publishing Company

(Supports Mostly Science magazine, pages 18–19) **Reading for a purpose; learning about food chains.** Students can read the story aloud with a partner. Check answers to Exercise B in class. For more work, have students rewrite the false statements as true. You may want to save this page in the student's **Assessment Portfolio.**

What Kind of Animal Is It?

Complete the graphic organizer. Use the animals on page 17 of your Mostly Science magazine. Put their names in the correct box. You may add the names of any other animals that you know.

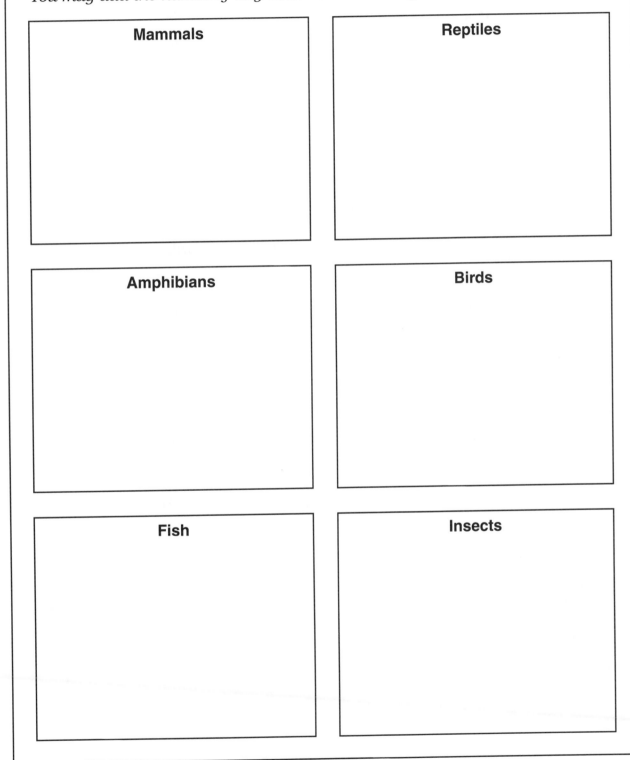

Mammals

Reptiles

Amphibians

Birds

Fish

Insects

(Supports Mostly Science magazine, pages 18–19) **Identifying animal names; filling in a chart.** Students can complete the page independently or with a partner. Have students compare their lists of animals. For more work, have students write a sentence about each animal in their graphic organizer.

Coyote

A. *Read each statement. Write **True** or **False** on the line.*

1. Coyote lived in the mountains. _____

2. Coyote was a star-watcher. _____

3. Coyote's best friend was Eagle. _____

4. Coyote wanted to climb up into the sky. _____

5. Coyote used branches to make a ladder. _____

6. Coyote was not happy on the moon. _____

7. Coyote decided to move the stars around. _____

8. Coyote made outlines of all his friends. _____

B. *Fill in the missing words. Use words from the Data Bank.*

Long ago, Coyote decided to climb up to the sky. He like the

_____, and he was also tired of the desert. He used _____

arrows to make a ladder. He climbed the ladder higher and _____.

Finally he reached the _____. Then he decided to _____

the stars around. Coyote shot his arrows _____ the stars and

moved them to different places in the _____. Some of the stars

made a shape like a _____. Other stars looked like a _____,

and many other animals. The sky was _____ of new

constellations.

DATA BANK

at	full	goat	move	some
bear	higher	moon	sky	stars

(Supports Mostly Science magazine, pages 20–23) **Reading comprehension; cloze exercise.** Students complete the page independently. Check answers in class. You may want to save this page in the student's **Assessment Portfolio.**

Capital Letters

We use a capital letter for the first letter of many words.
Examples:

The first word in a sentence
My sister is in the band.

The pronoun I
Kim and I will bring the snacks.

days and months
Monday, Tuesday July, August

names of people
Miguel, Mary, Mr. Concepción

languages and nationalities
Chinese, Spanish, Vietnamese

cities, countries, continents
Paris, Equador, Africa

Rewrite each of these sentences. Add capital letters where they belong.

1. tigers live in africa and asia.

_____

2. we like to eat lunch at the lake.

_____

3. i take piano lessons on monday with mr. yu.

_____

4. jose's birthday is in april.

_____

5. the united states is a powerful country.

_____

6. manuel and i are learning to speak chinese.

_____

(Supports Mostly Science magazine, pages 20–23) **Capital letters, spelling; syntax.** Students complete the page independently. Check answers in class. You may want to save this page in the student's **Assessment Portfolio.**

21

More About Coyotes

A. *Read more about coyotes.*

Coyotes are members of the dog family. They are smart and tricky. The Indians of the Southwest liked to tell stories about Coyote the trickster.

Adult coyotes are about the size of a large dog. Males weigh between 18 and 44 pounds. Females weigh between 15 and 20 pounds. Coyotes are usually gray. They have long ears. Their sense of smell is very strong. Coyotes talk to each other with loud, howling noises, especially at night.

Coyotes live in many different habitats. They can survive in the desert, the forest, and even in the cold tundra of Alaska and northern Canada. Coyotes eat mice, rabbits, birds, insects, and fruit. Sometimes they eat farm animals like chicken and sheep.

B. *Answer these questions about coyotes.*

1. What animal family do coyotes belong to?

_____

2. Who liked to tell stories about coyote the trickster?

_____

3. How much does an adult male coyote weigh?

_____

4. How do coyotes talk to each other?

_____

5. What do coyotes eat?

_____

(Supports Mostly Science magazine, pages 20–23) **Reading for a purpose; learning about coyotes; writing.**
Students can read the story aloud with a partner. Check answers to Exercise B in class. You may want to save this page in the student's **Assessment Portfolio.**

What Is the Moon?

For thousands of years, people on Earth looked up into the night sky and saw the beautiful moon. They all saw something different. Some saw a man's face. They called him the "man in the moon." Other people saw a rabbit or a house. There are many stories about what made the shapes that people saw in the moon.

A. *What do you see when you look at the moon? Draw a picture of what you see.*

B. *On another piece of paper, write a story about what you see in the moon.*

(Supports Mostly Science magazine, pages 20–23) **Imagery; process writing; expressing ideas through art.**
Display students' drawings in the classroom. Volunteers can read their stories to the class. Have students draft, edit, and revise their stories about the moon.

23

DATA COLLECTION

Sizes of the Moon

Materials:
piece of three-ring binder paper

A. *Observe and collect data.*

1. Watch for a full moon. The moon often looks very large when it first rises. As soon as you can see it, look at the moon through a hole in a three-ring binder paper.

2. Later, the moon will be higher in the sky. When it is, look at it again through the same hole in the paper. Does the moon look bigger? Does it look smaller? Does it look the same?

B. *Draw conclusions.*

Compare the size of the moon early in the evening and later. Write your conclusions on another piece of paper.

C. *Look at these two stars. Which one looks bigger to you. Draw a circle around the one that looks bigger.*

© Addison-Wesley Publishing Company

(Supports Mostly Science magazine, page 24) **Data collection; conducting an experiment; comparing and contrasting; measuring.** Students work with a partner to complete Exercises A and B. Have them compare their results with the rest of the class. In Exercise C, students can measure the stars after they have circled one.

More About Space

A. *Read about the solar system.*

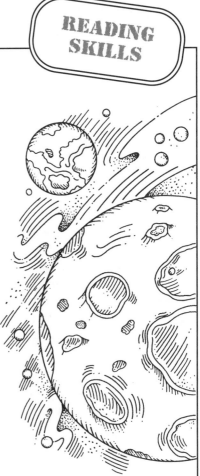

Our solar system has nine planets. They go around the sun. Their names are Mercury, Venus, Earth, Mars, Jupiter, Saturn, Uranus, Neptune, and Pluto. Some of these planets, like Earth, are hard balls of rock. Other planets are giant balls of gas—we think!

Jupiter is the biggest planet. It is more than 1,000 times bigger than Earth. It has at least four moons. You can see them through a telescope.

Pluto is the farthest planet from the sun. It is between 2,700 and 4,600 billion miles from the sun. You know that Earth goes around the sun once every year. Well, Pluto orbits the sun once every 248 years!

B. *Answer these questions about the solar system.*

1. What are the names of the nine planets?

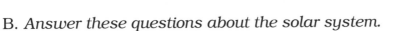

_____

2. How many moons around Jupiter can you see through a telescope?

_____

3. Which planet is farthest from the sun?

_____

4. How often does Earth orbit the sun?

_____

5. How often does Pluto go around the sun?

_____

(Supports Mostly Science magazine, page 25) **Reading for a purpose; learning about the planets.** Students can read the story aloud with a partner. Check answers to Exercise B in class. You may want to save this page in the student's **Assessment Portfolio.**

25

The Red Planet

A. *Read about our neighbor in the solar system.*

Mars is the fourth planet from the sun. It is one of Earth's neighbors in the sky. Mars is called the Red Planet. We know a lot about this planet.

Mars is a very windy place. Strong windstorms blow the red sand of Mars across the planet. Sometimes the wind quiets down, and the sandstorms stop. On the days when the wind is quiet, Mars has a temperature of about -9 degrees Fahrenheit. That's cold!

Like all the planets, Mars orbits the sun. It takes Mars 687 days to go around the sun once. It takes Earth only 365 days to orbit the sun. Mars rotates on its axis once every 24 hours and 37 minutes. That's about the same time it takes Earth to rotate.

Mars has the largest volcano in the solar system. The volcano is called Olympus Mons. Olympus Mons is 16 miles high. The largest volcano on Earth is only five miles high.

B. *Answer these questions about Mars.*

1. What is Mars called?

_____

2. What is the weather usually like on Mars?

_____

3. How long does it take Mars to orbit the sun?

_____

4. How long does it take Mars to rotate on its axis?

_____

5. What is the name of the volcano on Mars?

_____

(Supports Mostly Science magazine, page 26) **Reading for a purpose; learning about planets; writing.**
Students can read the story aloud with a partner. Check answers to Exercise B in class. You may want to save this page in the student's **Assessment Portfolio.**

Comets

A. *Read about comets that share the solar system with us.*

A comet is an icy object that travels around the sun. When a comet gets close to the sun, the ice begins to melt. The melting ice looks like a long tail that trails across the sky.

Halley's Comet is famous. It takes 76 years to travel around the sun. This comet is named for Edmond Halley. He saw the comet in 1682. He found out that the same comet passed Earth in 1531 and 1607. He predicted that the comet would return in 1758. He was right!

The last time Halley's Comet passed by Earth was in 1986. It will not appear in our sky again until 2061.

B. *Read each statement. Write **True** or **False** on the line.*

1. A comet is an icy object that travels around the sun. _____

2. A comet gets larger when it gets close to the sun. _____

3. The tail of a comet is made of gas. _____

4. Edmond Halley first saw his comet in 1682. _____

5. Halley predicted that the comet would return in 25 years. _____

6. Halley's Comet will appear next in the year 2061. _____

(Supports Mostly Science magazine, page 27) **Reading for a purpose; learning about planets.** Students can read the story aloud with a partner. Check answers to Exercise B in class. For more work, have students rewrite the false statements as true. You may want to save this page in the student's **Assessment Portfolio.**

27

People and Animals

A. *Animals are important in our lives. Fill in the graphic organizer.*
Identify some animals by their relationships to people. Identify
other animals by where they live. You may put the names of
some animals in more than one box.

Animals some people are afraid of	Animals that work for people

Pet animals	Farm animals

Animals that live in cities	Sea animals

B. *Choose three animals and write a sentence about each one.*

_____

_____

_____

(Supports Mostly Science magazine, page 28) **Home-School Connection; process writing; identifying animals; spelling.** Students can work independently or with a partner to complete the page. Have students share their lists with the class. For more work, have students think of other animal categories. Have students take this page home to share with their families.

Dinosaurs

A. *Read about life on Earth long ago.*

Dinosaurs lived on earth for about 165 million years. They belonged to the reptile family.

Some dinosaurs, like the Compsognathus, were as small as chickens. They ate insects. Other dinosaurs were huge, like the Allosaurus. It was 39 feet long, and it ate other dinosaurs. Some dinosaurs ate only plants.

The dinosaurs died out about 64 million years ago. No one knows for sure what killed them. Some scientists believe that a giant meteor hit Earth. Others believe that the weather became too warm for the dinosaurs. The dinosaurs lived and died long before there were any humans on Earth to see them.

B. *Read each statement. Write **True** or **False** on the line.*

1. Dinosaurs were reptiles. _____

2. All dinosaurs were large. _____

3. People always knew about dinosaurs. _____

4. The Compsognathus was bigger than the Allosaurus. _____

5. Dinosaurs ate humans. _____

6. No one knows for sure why all the dinosaurs died. _____

(Supports Mostly Science magazine, page 29) **Reading for a purpose; learning about dinosaurs.** Students can read the story aloud with a partner. Check answers to Exercise B in class. For more work, have students rewrite the false statements as true. You may want to save this page in the student's **Assessment Portfolio.**

29

A Trip into Space

Write your own poem about a trip into space. What planets will you visit? What will you do there? Share your poem with the class.

(Supports Mostly Science magazine, page 30) **Home-School Connection; writing a poem; imagery.**
Volunteers can read their poems to the class. Display the poems in the classroom. You may want to save a copy of this page in the student's **Assessment Portfolio.** Have students take a copy of this page home to share with their families.

A. *Listen to the song "Listen to the Raindrops." Fill in the missing words.*

Chorus

Listen to the _____ falling down;

Listen to the raindrops on the _____;

Listen _____ the raindrops falling down,

_____ down.

First verse

Now, I look _____ my window,

And I smell the _____, clean air;

The _____, they sway so gently;

And the _____ lies everywhere;

And it _____ so good just

To hear the sound so _____.

Second verse

_____ in the city or the country,

You could be _____ on the back porch stairs;

Friends and family around _____

_____ silently aware—

As you sit and _____

And _____ the sound so clear.

B. *Do you like rain? Tell why or why not.*

_____

_____

_____

(Supports Mostly Science magazine, page 31) **Learning a song; cloze exercise; expressing opinions.**
Students complete the page independently. Check answers in class.

31

HOW ARE YOU DOING?

Now I Can	yes	no	not sure
1. talk about beavers			
2. design a symmetrical symbol			
3. use -er and -est to show comparison			
4. choose the correct homophone			
5. do an experiment with ice			
6. retell a story in sequence			
7. use more and most to show comparison			
8. talk about the solar system			
9. use capital letters correctly			
10. write a poem about space			

Now I Know	In My Language	yes	no	not sure
branches				
claws				
disk				
elephant				
habitat				
hair				
heart				
loud				
magnet				
mud				
planet				
pole				
pond				
rocket				
shallow				

____ Teacher Check

(Supports Mostly Science magazine) **Home-School Connection; self-assessment, vocabulary development.** Students fill in the grids about what they have learned in this magazine. In the bottom grid, suggest that students write each vocabulary word in their native language in the blank column. You may want to save this page in the student's **Assessment Portfolio.** Have students take a copy of this page home to share with their family members.

SKILLS JOURNAL

1

Charles Skidmore
Anne Marie Drayton

CONTENTS

Mostly Social Studies Skills Journal   3–32

(To accompany student pages 3–32)

• •

Featuring:

A Publication of the World Language Division

Director of Product Development: Judith M. Bittinger

Executive Editor: Elinor Chamas

Editorial Development: Kathleen M. Smith

Text and Cover Design: Taurins Design Associates

Art Direction and Production: Taurins Design Associates

Production and Manufacturing: James W. Gibbons

Illustrators: Andrew Christie 22; Sue Miller 4, 12; Chris Reed 13, 15, 24, 27; Mena Dolobowsky 28; Dave Sullivan 32

• •

Find the Names

A. *Names are different around the world. Find the first names in this puzzle. Make a list to show which are girls' names and which are boys' names.*

```
Y N I M A R I S O L A Q N F I L
V I L H D O M I N I C P F R E H
E D P L O J V M L D A N G E L A
T O H D H W O E A L H J Q D K T
T C N E H N A N R R D E Q D E Y
E K E I S H A R A O V A G I G R
F T P A B L O N D T N I V E J O
A J A A N G B E C C H I N I K N
F H E N O M D L O Y B A C C D E
O M O M Y J K I F H C P N A A J
G A J P T A J Z M J I A M N M A
D A H L H K J A I L D L A O A D
N G M B O R F B C A L I R C R A
F K O J M D U E O I D C I O C M
I D O E A K E T B G E Q E K O I
N H D Q S H M H H M L I B F K E
```

ADAM	ELIZABETH	MARIE	TANYA
ANGELA	FREDDIE	MARISOL	THOMAS
BILL	HOWARD	MARVIN	TYRONE
DAVID	JONATHAN	NANCY	VERONICA
DIANA	KEISHA	PABLO	YVETTE
DOMINIC	MARCO	RUTH	

B. *Make a word search puzzle like the one on this page for the names of the students in your class. Make sure that you have everyone's name spelled correctly in your word search puzzle.*

(Supports Mostly Social Studies magazine) **Solving a puzzle; name recognition; socializing.** Students can work individually or in pairs to solve Exercise A. Check in class. You may want to list boys' and girls' names on the board. For Exercise B, you may want to list all students' names, then have students work in small groups to create their word search puzzles.

3

Where Do You Live?

When someone asks, "Where do you live?" there can be many answers. Read these answers.

Where do you live?

I live in the United States.

I live in Texas.

I live in Dallas.

The question "Where do you live?" has so many different answers because people like to divide the world into many parts. The same land can be a continent, a country, a state, a city, and a neighborhood.

Complete the graphic organizer about where you live.

Where I Live
Continent _____
Country_____
State_____
City_____
Neighborhood_____
Address _____

(Supports Mostly Social Studies magazine, page 4) **Home-School Connection; conversation; identifying place names.** Students can work individually or in pairs to complete the graphic organizer. You may want to have them practice conversations by making questions out of the information in the box. Have students take this page home to share with their families.

What Country Are You From?

A. *Find out what countries your classmates are from. First, collect the data.*

Name	Country of Origin

B. *Make a bar graph with the information.*

(Supports Mostly Social Studies magazine, page 5) **Home-School Connection; interviewing; data collection; graphing.** You may want to show students an example of a bar graph. Encourage students to talk about what their bar graphs show about the variety of countries of origin in the class. You may want to save this page in the student's **Assessment Portfolio**. Have students take a copy of this page home to share with their families.

Customs and Culture

The Baci Ceremony is an example of an important custom in the Laotian culture. Customs are things that many people from the same place believe in. They practice customs at special times and on special holidays.

A. *Use the graphic organizer to write about a family or a cultural custom that you know about. Then share it with your class.*

Name of custom	Time when we practice it

What we do	Why we do it

B. *Now write a paragraph that tells about your custom.*

_____

_____

_____

_____

(Supports Mostly Social Studies magazine, page 6) **Home-School Connection; appreciating different cultures; organizing information; process writing**. Give students time to ask their families about customs, if necessary. Have volunteers read their paragraphs aloud in Exercise B. You may want to save this page in the student's **Assessment Portfolio**. Have students take a copy of this page home to share with their families.

6

Valentine's Day

Valentine's Day is February 14 each year. It is a day for people to show their love and affection for each other.

On this day people send beautiful cards with loving messages to each other. Often in schools, students and teachers decorate a Valentine box with hearts and flowers. Each student puts valentine cards in this box for the other students in the class.

Adults also exchange gifts with their special loved ones. Cards, flowers, boxes of candy, and jewelry are popular items. People give these to express affection. Many people do this on Valentine's Day.

A. *Write the answers to these questions on another piece of paper.*
   1. When is Valentine's Day?
   2. What do people do on Valentine's Day?
   3. What are some popular Valentine's Day gifts?
   4. Why do people like Valentine's Day?
   5. Do you celebrate Valentine's Day in your home country?

B. *Make a Valentine's Day card in this space.*

(Supports Mostly Social Studies magazine, page 7) **Reading comprehension; expressing ideas through art.** Students complete the page independently. If they do this page near Valentine's Day, display their cards in the classroom.

7

It Happened Yesterday

Use the **past tense** to show that an action happened an hour ago, yesterday, last week, or some other time in the past.

Examples: Yonaira <u>stayed</u> after school yesterday.
My sister and I <u>washed</u> the dishes.

A. *Study the verbs in this chart.*

Regular verbs form the past tense by adding *-ed.*		**Irregular verbs** have special past tense forms.	
verb	**past tense**	**verb**	**past tense**
help	helped	begin	began
learn	learned	come	came
start	started	give	gave
play	played	see	saw
work	worked	tell	told

B. *Practice the past tense. Write a sentence with each of the past tense verbs in the chart. Use another piece of paper if you need more space.*

_____

_____

_____

_____

_____

_____

_____

_____

_____

(Supports Mostly Social Studies magazine, pages 8–9) **Past tense, spelling.** Students can work independently or with a partner. Have them share their sentences with the class.

Major United States Cities

Washington, D.C. is the capital of the United States. The federal government is located there. The United States has many other important cities. Look at the map to see some other important U.S. cities.

Continental United States

On another piece of paper, answer these questions about the map.

1. Is Washington, D.C. on the East Coast or the West Coast?
2. Is Philadelphia north or south of Washington, D.C.?
3. Is Miami north or south of Washington, D.C.?
4. Which city is closer to Washington, D.C., Atlanta or Denver?
5. Which city is further from Washington, D.C., Boston or Boise?
6. Is Phoenix north or south of San Francisco?
7. Name two cities on the West Coast.
8. Name a city in the Northwest.
9. Name a city in the Southwest.
10. Name a city in the Southeast.

(Supports Mostly Social Studies magazine, pages 8–9) **Reading a map; learning U.S. city names; understanding compass directions.** Students complete the page independently. Check in class.

9

School Rules

What are some important rules that students need to follow in a classroom?

A. *Work with a partner and write three important classroom rules. Share your rules with the class.*

1. _____

   _____

2. _____

   _____

3. _____

   _____

Now think about rules for being a success in school. What are some important rules to follow about doing your school work?

B. *Work with a partner and write three important rules for being a successful student. Share your rules with the class.*

1. _____

   _____

2. _____

   _____

3. _____

   _____

C. *Read your rules in Exercises A and B. Do you follow these rules? Check off the answer that is true for you.*

_____ I follow these rules all the time.

_____ I follow these rules most of the time.

_____ I don't follow these rules. I need to change my behavior.

(Supports Mostly Social Studies magazine, page 10) **Home-School Connection; writing rules; awareness of responsibility.** Some suggestions: Exercise A—don't jump ahead in line; listen when someone else is talking; Exercise B—make enough time for studying every day; ask questions in class. Post a few of the most appropriate rules somewhere in the classroom. Have students take this page home to share with their families.

Good Habits

*Here are some things that people do. Some things are good and
some are not. In the chart below, write the items in the list in the
column where they belong. Add your own ideas to each list.*

wear seat belts in a car
listen to others when they are
   talking
waste paper
eat lots of fruit and vegetables
throw papers in the street
be kind to animals

learn CPR
write on walls of buildings
waste water
wait your turn
interrupt people when they are
   talking
exercise every day

Do	Don't

(Supports Mostly Social Studies magazine, page 11) **Understanding imperatives; listing dos and don'ts;
awareness of responsibility.** Students can work independently or with a partner to complete the page.
Encourage discussion about the *Don'ts* that students list and how to correct them.

Punctuation Poems

What are punctuation marks? They are marks that tell you to

. ? , ' " " !

stop ask pause short'n "speak" exclaim

1. the PERIOD .
   At the end of a thought,
   Sign off with this dot.

2. the QUESTION MARK ?
   Is there something you must
   ask?
   Make this mark—it's your task.

3. the COMMA ,
   When you write,
   Use the comma because
   It gives your reader a chance to
   pause.

4. the APOSTROPHE '
   An apostrophe shows who owns
   a thing,
   Like *Marco's* hat or a *girl's* ring.
   This mark also shrinks words—
   do not into *don't*,
   Or *will not* into *won't*.

5. QUOTATION MARKS " "
   To find out who says what,
   Look at the pair of marks you've
   got.
   "Who's there?" asked Ben.
   "It's me," said Brigitte.

6. EXCLAMATION MARK !
   If you want to scare or excite,
   This is the mark that you
   should write!

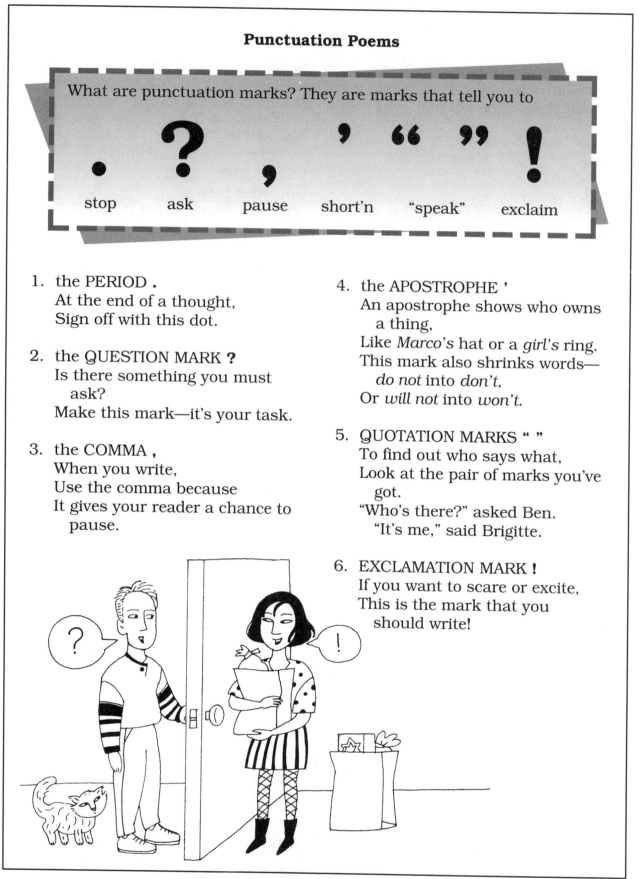

Space Pirates

Read the story aloud with a partner. One of you will read the words. The other will read the punctuation marks. Follow the code at the bottom of the page.

"Yikes!" cried Pirate Pat, sitting in her rocket. "Thunder and lightening! There's a treasure spaceship. Look lively, my mates!"

"How far away is the ship?" asked the pirate captain.

"We'll meet the ship before the sun sets," said Pirate Pat. "What are your orders, captain?"

"Mates! Listen!" called the captain. "Put up a false flag. Stay well hidden. When we're almost upon them, we'll raise our flag. Raise the pirate flag! That'll be a beautiful surprise, hey?" And he laughed a deep, mean, nasty, chilling, scary, gruesome, eerie, wild, awful, terrifying, pirate laugh!

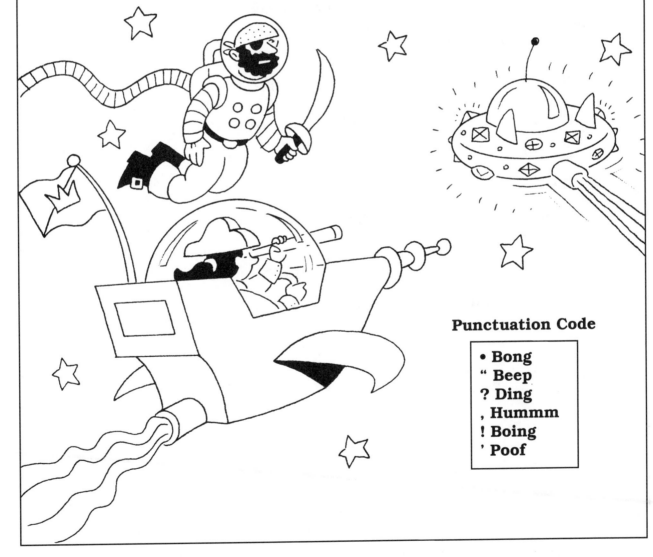

Punctuation Code

- • Bong
- " Beep
- ? Ding
- , Hummm
- ! Boing
- ' Poof

(Supports Mostly Social Studies magazine, pages 12–13) **Punctuation; syntax.** Encourage students to give animated readings of the story. For additional practice, have them name the marks of punctuation in the box.

13

READING SKILLS

Native American Food

A. *Read about the food that ancient California Indians ate.*

As long as 10,000 years ago, Indians lived in the area known as California today. These ancient Indians lived off the land and the sea. They spent much of their time looking for food.

Acorns were one of their most important foods. Most Indian tribes lived near oak groves. They got acorns from the oak trees that grew in the oak grove. The women had the job of gathering acorns and turning them into flour.

The California Indians also ate meat. They hunted for deer, rabbit, and raccoon. They used bows and arrows and traps to catch the wild animals. Then they roasted the meat over a fire.

Many Indians lived near the coast. They gathered shellfish, like clams and mussels, from the ocean. Most Indians fished from the shore. Some Indians went out into the ocean in boats to fish.

B. *Read each statement. Write **True** or **False** on the line.*

1. The Indians settled in California 10,000 years ago. _____

2. The Indians got acorns by digging in the ground. _____

3. The Indians were not meat eaters. _____

4. They caught wild animals with bows and arrows and traps. _____

5. Many Indians gathered shellfish from the ocean. _____

6. They always fished from the shore. _____

(Supports Mostly Social Studies magazine, pages 14–15) **Reading for a purpose; learning about Indian food.** Students can read the story aloud with a partner. Check answers to Exercise B in class. For more work, have students rewrite the false statements as true. You may want to save this page in the student's **Assessment Portfolio.**

Personal Timeline

You can use a timeline to map out the important things that are part of your own history.

A. *Fill in these blanks about your history.*

year I was born _____   year I started school _____

year I began to walk and talk _____   year I moved to a new place _____

years my brothers and sisters were   other important events and the

born _____   years _____

Ask your family to help you with the dates in the list above. When you finish your list, you are ready to make your timeline.

B. *Make a timeline of your life. Follow the example below.*

1. Draw a line across a big piece of paper.
2. Write the year you were born under the line.
4. Write "Year I was born" above the line.
5. Fill in the rest of the timeline. Use information from your list above.
6. Decorate your timeline.
7. Share your timeline with the class.

Year I was born   Year I started school   Year we moved to Texas

Year I walked   Year my sister   Year my team
and talked   was born   won soccer
          championship

1983   1985   1988   1992   1993   1995

(Supports Mostly Social Studies magazine, pages 14–15) **Home-School Connection; making a timeline; understanding chronology.** Give students time to ask their families to help them with dates and events. Volunteers can tell the class the story of their lives as they show their timelines. Display the timelines in the classroom. Have students take this page home to share with their families.

Create Your Own Map

Design and draw your own country. Include as many of the features in the list below as you can. These features are shown on the map on pages 16 and 17 of your Mostly Social Studies magazine. Label the features.

bay	gulf	peninsula
cape	island	plains
coast	lake	plateau
desert	mountain	river
forest	ocean	valley

(Supports Mostly Social Studies magazine, pages 16–17) **Geographical terms; learning through art.** Help students research any geographical terms they don't understand. Have volunteers use their maps to tell the class about their countries. Display the maps in the classroom. You may want to save this page in the student's **Assessment Portfolio**.

Color the Map

A. *Use at least five different colored pencils, crayons, or markers to color the states on this map of the United States. First, use a pencil to lightly write the name of the color you will use on each state. Check that you are not using the same color for states that share a border. Then color your map.*

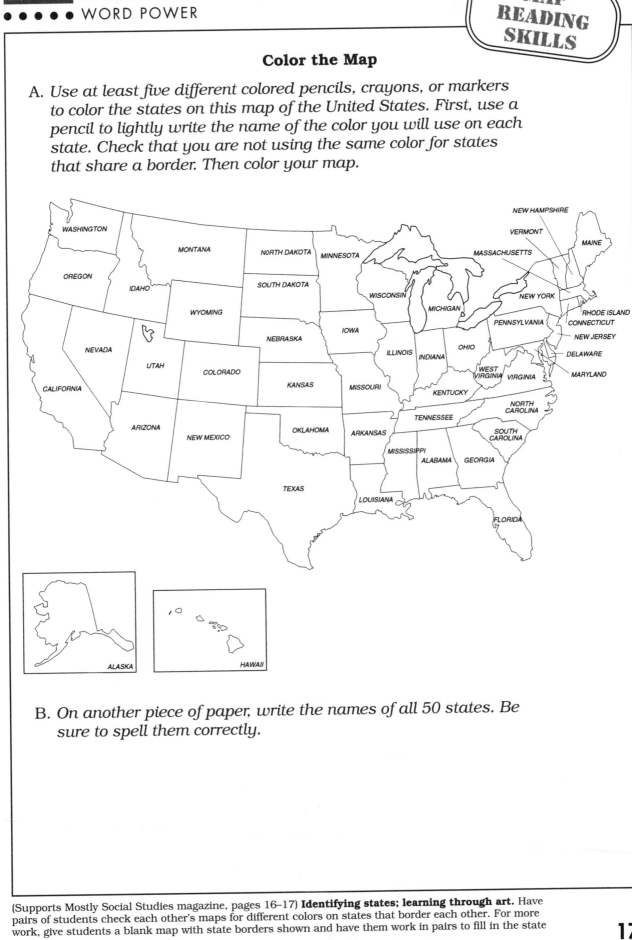

B. *On another piece of paper, write the names of all 50 states. Be sure to spell them correctly.*

(Supports Mostly Social Studies magazine, pages 16–17) **Identifying states; learning through art.** Have pairs of students check each other's maps for different colors on states that border each other. For more work, give students a blank map with state borders shown and have them work in pairs to fill in the state names.

Story Questions

A. *Answer these questions about "Phaeton and the Chariot of the Sun."*

1. Who was the god of the sun?

_____

2. What did Apollo do every morning?

_____

3. What did the people on Earth see?

_____

4. Why couldn't Phaeton drive the chariot?

_____

5. What happened when the horses pulled the chariot high up into the sky?

_____

6. What happened when the chariot went down close to Earth?

_____

7. Who is Zeus?

_____

8. How did Zeus stop Phaeton?

_____

B. *Myths always explain something. What does this myth try to explain? Circle the correct letter.*

a. why the oceans are so deep and salty

b. why mountain are so tall

c. how the deserts and tundra were made

d. how the sun moves from east to west

(Supports Mostly Social Studies magazine, pages 18–19) **Reading for a purpose; understanding myths.** Students should reread the story before they do this page. Check answers in class. You may want to save this page in the student's **Assessment Portfolio.**

To, Too, Two

The words **to, too,** and **two** sound the same, but they have different meanings.

to: in the direction of   *I am going <u>to</u> the store.*

too: very   *The horses were <u>too</u> strong for Phaeton to control.*

two: the number 2   *I have <u>two</u> friends in the Philippines.*

Complete these sentences. Write the correct word in the blank.

to   too   two

1. Do you have _____ dollars that I can borrow?

2. It is _____ cold to play outside today.

3. I am going _____ New York City next week.

4. Will you come _____ my house on Saturday?

5. The homework was _____ hard for me!

6. We have _____ security guards in the cafeteria.

7. I am going _____ the principal's office now.

8. Do you think my composition is _____ long?

9. That class is _____ noisy.

10. Mark has _____ dogs and a cat.

11. My aunt went _____ London on a business trip.

12. I have _____ pairs of skates. They are both _____ small.

13. My dad took my bicycle _____ the repair shop.

14. Miguel gave Nancy _____ goldfish for her birthday.

15. Ramon went _____ the movies with his _____ friends.

(Supports Mostly Social Studies magazine, pages 18–19) **To, too, two; spelling; syntax.** Students complete the page independently. Check answers in class. You may want to save this page in the student's **Assessment Portfolio.**

19

Past Tense Practice

> The **past tense** of a verb shows that an action happened yesterday, last week, or some other time in the past. Regular verbs add *-ed* to show the past tense.
>
> **Examples:** look<u>ed</u>   walk<u>ed</u>   pull<u>ed</u>

A. *Complete each sentence by adding -ed to the verb in parentheses to form the past tense. Write the past tense of the verb on the line. Write the whole sentence on another piece of paper.*

1. David and Alan _____ chess with their grandfather. (play)

2. The shapes _____ CD and Byte in one adventure. (attack)

3. The skunk _____ its awful smell under the house. (spray)

4. A big problem _____ for CD and Byte in the last story. (wait)

5. The girls _____ more than 70 different flags at the show. (count)

6. John Chapman _____ rivers and climbed mountains. (cross)

7. Paul _____ the decimals with his calculator. (add)

8. The donkey _____ the horse to carry some packages. (ask)

9. Phaeton _____ to drive the chariot of the sun. (want)

10. John Chapman _____ many apple seeds. (plant)

B. *On another piece of paper, write a sentence using each of these verbs in the past tense.*

appear	clean	reach
burn	fold	start
chew	look	subtract

© Addison-Wesley Publishing Company

Words That Pronouns Refer To

Pronouns take the place of nouns. Some common pronouns are

I   you   he   she   it   we   they   me   him   her   us   them

A pronoun refers back to a person or thing already mentioned in a sentence.

Example: _Linh and I_ cleaned out the art room closet. _We_ stayed after school to do it.

The pronoun _we_ refers back to _Linh and I_.

Tell what each underlined pronoun refers to in the sentences below. Write the person, place, or thing on the line. Follow the example.

Example:
I wore my new shoes today. <u>They</u> hurt my feet.   <u>new shoes</u>

1. John Chapman loved the outdoors. <u>He</u> walked across many states in America.

2. Johnny loved the wild animals in the forest. He wanted to protect <u>them</u>.

3. Johnny Appleseed gave seeds to everyone he met. People across America planted <u>them</u>.

4. Some of the apple trees that grew from Johnny's apple seeds are still alive today. <u>They</u> are large, old trees.

5. The Mayan Indians built this pyramid in 250 AD. <u>It</u> is more than 1,700 years old.

6. Columbus arrived in the Americas in 1492. The Indians came to the Americas thousands of years before <u>him</u>.

7. The U.S. Senate has 100 senators. <u>They</u> are elected every six years.

8. The police detective used fingerprints to solve the crime. <u>She</u> showed the fingerprints in court.

1. _____

2. _____

3. _____

4. _____

5. _____

6. _____

7. _____

8. _____

(Supports Mostly Social Studies magazine, pages 20–23) **Pronouns; pronoun referents; syntax.** Students complete the page independently. Check in class. You may want to save this page in the student's **Assessment Portfolio**.

Rivers, Lakes, and Mountains

Look at the map. Read the names of the rivers, lakes, mountains, and other geographical features.

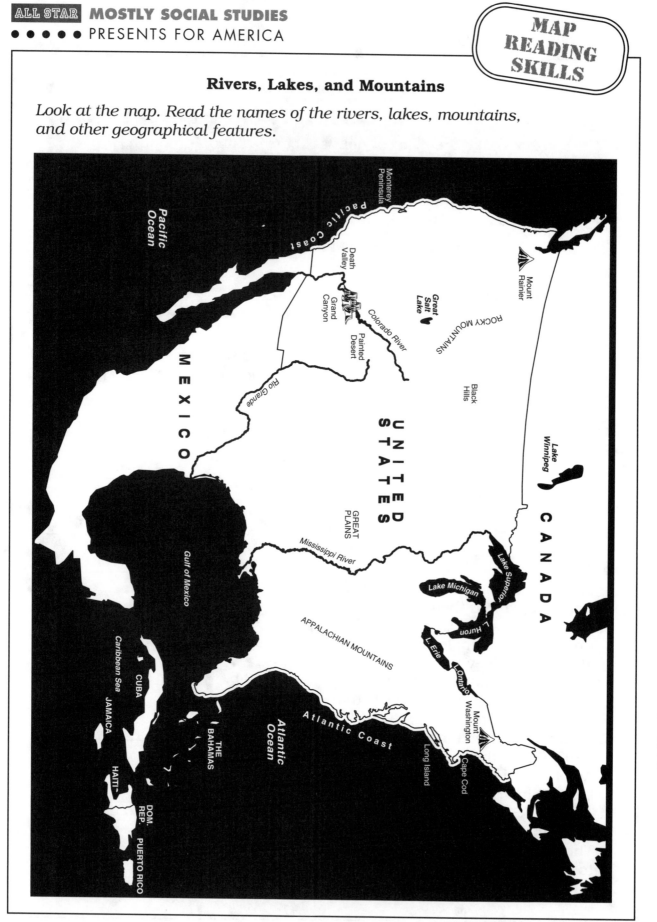

(Supports Mostly Social Studies magazine, pages 20–23) **Geographical features; reading a map; understanding compass directions.** With a partner or in a small group, have students read aloud the names of the geographical features on the map.

Writing Geographical Terms

Use the map on page 22 to find examples of the following geographical terms. Write their names in the boxes.

Mountains	Rivers
Plains	**Lakes**
Oceans	**Other features**

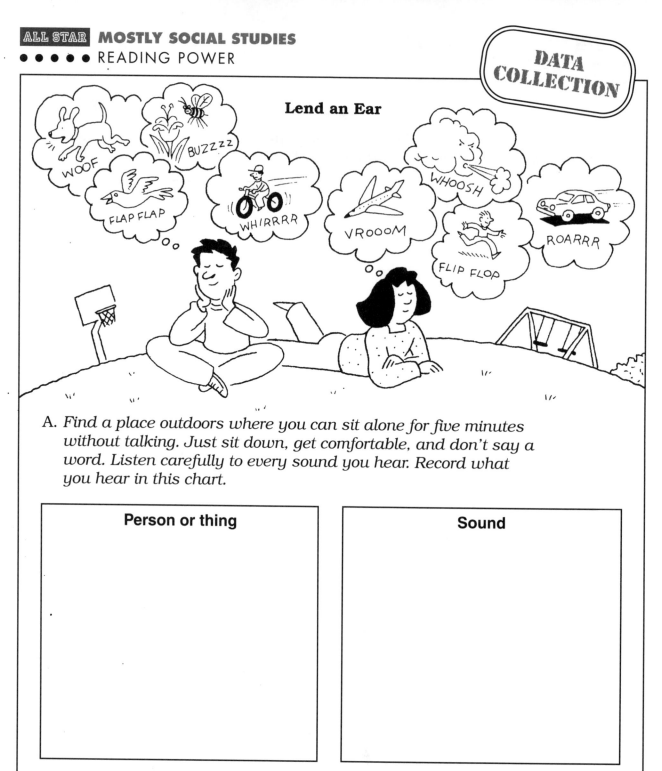

Lend an Ear

A. *Find a place outdoors where you can sit alone for five minutes without talking. Just sit down, get comfortable, and don't say a word. Listen carefully to every sound you hear. Record what you hear in this chart.*

Person or thing	Sound

B. *Now go the same place outdoors and sit alone again. This time close your eyes for five minutes and listen to every sound. Are the sounds louder with your eyes closed?*

C. *Compare your list in Exercise A with a friend's list. Did both of you hear the same sounds?*

(Supports Mostly Social Studies magazine, page 24) **Learning about senses; data collection; comparing/contrasting.** If it's not possible to go outdoors for this experiment, choose an indoor place, such as the cafeteria, the gym, or the art room. You may want to have students compare their charts as a class.

Plan a Healthful Meal

Instead of this: . . . . Eat this:	
doughnut . . . . toast and jam	
fried chicken . . . . baked chicken	
ice cream . . . . frozen fruit bar	
french fries . . . . baked potato	
whole milk . . . . skim milk	
potato chips . . . . pretzels	

A. *Write down some healthful foods you can eat for these meals.*

Breakfast

_____

_____

Lunch

_____

_____

Dinner

_____

_____

Snacks

_____

_____

B. *What's your favorite food?*

_____

_____

_____

_____

(Supports Mostly Social Studies magazine, page 25) **Home-School Connection; learning about healthful foods; making lists; expressing opinions.** Students complete the page independently, then share their ideas with the class. Have students take this page home to share with their families.

25

Speedwalker

Imagine that you can walk at the speed of ten miles per hour (mph). The states below give the number of miles across in the longest direction. On the lines, write how long it would take to walk across each state.

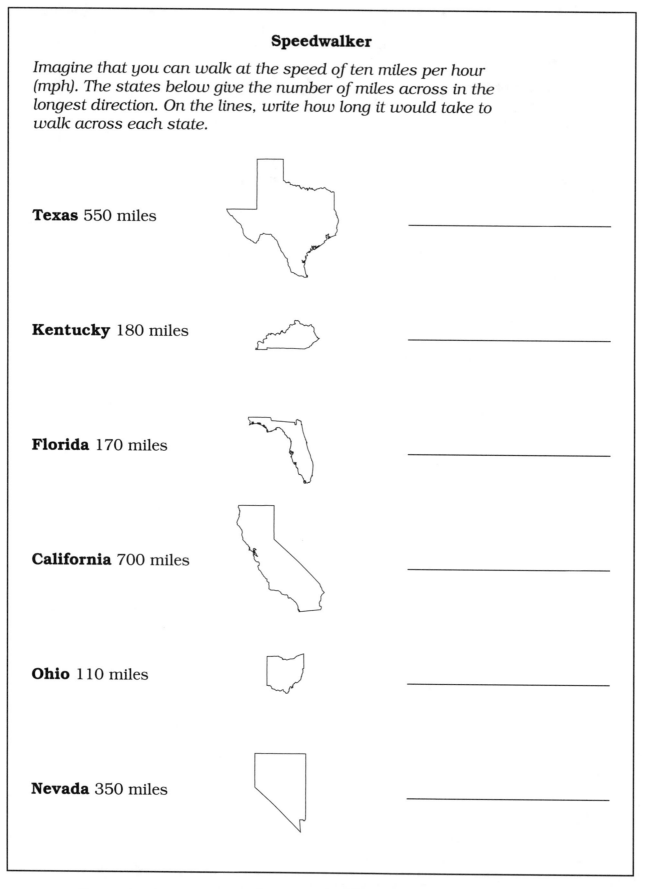

Texas 550 miles   _____

Kentucky 180 miles   _____

Florida 170 miles   _____

California 700 miles   _____

Ohio 110 miles   _____

Nevada 350 miles   _____

(Supports Mostly Social Studies magazine, page 26) **Math skills: division; reviewing state names.** Students complete the page independently. Check in class. For more work, have students calculate how long it would take to walk across the states using different rates of walking.

Recycle Fun

How many ways can you think of to recycle a two-liter plastic soda bottle? Draw or write your ideas in this box.

(Supports Mostly Social Studies magazine, page 27) **Home-School Connection; expressing ideas through art; environmental awareness.** You may want to have students talk in pairs or small groups about their ideas for recycling. Students complete the page independently. Display drawings or written ideas in the classroom. You may want to save this page in the student's **Assessment Portfolio.** Have students take a copy of this page home to share with their families.

High Flyers

Here's a story about another famous invention.
Read the paragraphs and answer the questions.

Orville and Wilbur Wright were brothers from Ohio. They spent a lot of time watching birds. They studied how birds move their wings when they fly. Then Orville and Wilbur built a plane.

On December 14, 1903, they tried to take off from Kill Devil Hill in North Carolina. The plane didn't get off the ground. But three days later, Orville flew the plane for twelve seconds.

On the same day, they made three more flights. The longest was 59 seconds. It was five more years before anyone else kept a plane in the air for more than a minute. By that time, the Wright brothers were flying for more than an hour at a time!

1. Where were the Wright brothers from?

   _____

2. What did the Wright brothers study?

   _____

3. When did they fly an airplane for the first time?

   _____

4. How many flights did the Wright brothers make the first day?

   _____

5. How long was it before other people made longer flights?

   _____

(Supports Mostly Social Studies magazine, page 28) **Reading for a purpose; writing.** Students can read the page aloud and answer the questions with a partner or as a class. You may want to save this page in the student's **Assessment Portfolio**.

Classroom Hall of Fame

A. *Interview a partner. Ask what special talent he or she has. What interesting or exciting event happened in his or her life? Make notes on another piece of paper.*

B. *Now design a poster about your partner that tells about a special thing you found out in your interview. Here are some ideas that you could illustrate:*

has lived in the most places

has an interesting pet

had the funniest experience in school

looks like a famous person

good dancer

kindest person

has the most brothers and sisters

super basketball player

Draw your poster in the space below. If you want, use a photo of your partner. Under the poster, write one or two sentences that tell what makes your partner special.

Partner's name _____

_____

_____

_____

(Supports Mostly Social Studies magazine, page 29) **Interviewing; note-taking; appreciating special talents; imagery; expressing ideas through art.** Encourage students to be imaginative with their posters. Display them in the classroom. Volunteers can give oral presentations of their posters to the class.

29

Handprint Poem

*Trace your hand in the space below. Then write a poem about
yourself that fits the shape of the palm and the fingers. Share
your poem with the class.*

(Supports Mostly Social Studies magazine, page 30) **Home-School Connection; writing a poem; learning
through art.** Your students may benefit from working in pairs or small groups to brainstorm ideas for their
poems. Display the poems in the classroom. You may want to save this page in the student's **Assessment
Portfolio**. Have students take a copy of this page home to share with their families.

Write a Song

Write your own song and illustrate it.

This _____ is your _____.

This _____ is my _____.

From _____ to the _____.

From the _____ _____.

To the _____ _____.

This _____ was made for you and me.

(Supports Mostly Social Studies magazine, page 31) **Rewriting a song; learning language through song.**
After students have enjoyed "This Land Is Your Land," point out that you can change key words and make a
new song about your town, your classroom, or your school. Students work with a partner to make the substi-
tutions. Volunteers can share their new songs with the class.

HOW ARE YOU DOING?

Now I Can	yes	no	not sure
1. interview a partner			
2. tell what continent, country, state, and city I live in			
3. find some important U.S. cities on a map			
4. list some school rules			
5. use punctuation correctly			
6. make a timeline of my life			
7. form the past tense with *-ed*			
8. tell what word a pronoun refers to			
9. plan a healthful meal			
10. solve division problems			

Now I Know	In My Language	yes	no	not sure
bananas				
born				
continent				
custom				
deserts				
dreams				
east				
fingerprint				
honored				
north				
rules				
snacks				
snow				
south				
west				

_____ Teacher Check

(Supports Mostly Social Studies magazine) **Home-School Connection; self-assessment, vocabulary development.** Students fill in the grids about what they have learned in this magazine. In the bottom grid, suggest that students write each vocabulary word in their native language in the blank column. You may want to save this page in the student's **Assessment Portfolio**. Have students take a copy of this page home to share with their family members.